D1621359

# NEWS OUT OF SCOTLAND

# NEWS OUT OF SCOTLAND

*Being a Miscellaneous Collection of Verse
and Prose, Sacred and Profane,
from the XIV to the
XVIII Century*

*Compiled and Annotated
by*
ELEANOR M. BROUGHAM

" *Je n'enseigne poinct, je raconte.*"
MONTAIGNE

LONDON
WILLIAM HEINEMANN LTD
1926

*First Published*, 1926

PRINTED IN GREAT BRITAIN BY THE WHITEFRIARS PRESS, LTD.
LONDON AND TONBRIDGE.

# DEDICATED
## TO
# LORD COLEBROOKE

*" I am willing to flatter myself with hopes that, by collecting these papers, I am not preparing for my future life either shame or repentance."*—Dr. Johnson.

# PREFACE

WHEN we consider the rich and varied dialect of Lowland Scotch, the first feature that strikes us is the French element, which distinguishes it sharply from the dialects of the north of England, and is accounted for by the early intercourse existing between France and Scotland. In 1069 Malcolm Canmore married a Saxon wife, Margaret, sister of Edgar the Atheling. Conditions were changing fast. The country was becoming feudal, and thanks to the influence of this pious and erudite Queen, the Romish Church had finally been established. For it is recorded that her skilful arguments alone won over the Culdee priests on such points as the Easter Communion and the observance of Sunday. She built, too, a stately church at Dunfermline, and refounded Iona. Meanwhile, the old Celtic tongue was discouraged at court, and its last echoes were dying away. Suddenly into this primitive world migrated whole families of Norman origin, bringing their language and their literature with them. They spread themselves everywhere, and in the twelfth century we find the Kings of Scotland issuing writs " *Scotis*, *Anglis et Francis* " to their Gaelic, Anglian and Norman French subjects. This invasion had far-reaching and beneficial results, for the people began to speak differently, adopting the unfamiliar vocabulary of these foreigners and mingling new and harmonious idioms with their rude and imperfect speech. And although eight centuries have passed since they came from over the water in their brightly-painted boats, we still hear some of their characteristic words—such as *flours, asters, ashet* and *jigot*—in common use north of the Tweed.

The earliest Scottish poetry is a somewhat stern and crude narrative of chivalry and quasi-historical deeds, and it is not until the beginning of the fifteenth century that a softer mood steals in. James I. and Robert Henryson, both inspired by Petrarch and Chaucer, added a fresh string to their lyres, and express a joy in nature which was absent from the harsh lines of their predecessors. New literary forms were introduced. Pastorals, allegories, satires and ballads sprang into being, and this sudden wave of vitality prepared the way for the splendid diction and immense variety of Dunbar. From that time forward the Northern muse was powerfully affected by England, although owing to political circumstances some poets preferred Latin and French to " Southron " as a source from which to supply their native dialect. Apt young scholars, eager for culture, wandered abroad and studied at foreign schools—

> " *One runneth to Almayne, another into Fraunce,*
> *To Paris, Padua, Lombardy, or Spain ;*
> *Another to Bonony, Rome or Orleaunce,*
> *To Cayns, to Thoulouse, Athens or Colayne* "

—returning home to brood over the classics, and in many cases producing cramped Mediæval versions of the ancient stories. They liked to associate their names with Homer or Virgil. The achievement of a successful translation conferred on a man a kind of reflected glory. And because they presented the great originals in forms congenial to their times, with sly allusions to everyday life and manners, they appealed instantly and directly to a large class of people and were eagerly read. Gawin Douglas, the learned poet-Bishop of Dunkeld, is justly famous as being the first translator of the Aeneid into any British tongue. Here is a landmark in scholarship, and a masterpiece which holds us still, for it echoes the impressiveness and authority of the great Mantuan himself.

This dawn of literary activity presents a striking contrast to the history of the times. Scotland at that period was a land of gloom and misery, full of animosity and party feuds. It was incredibly poor, and not without reason did an anonymous monk refer to it as " ane den of thieves," for acts of violence were committed with impunity, and the people were inured to oppression. There was robbery. There was " poysoun, manslaughtre, and mordre in sundry wyse." And over it all brooded the old enmity with England.

Perpetual fighting was in every sense prejudicial to the country, draining off, as it did, both treasure and population. Consequently progress was arrested. But from the day when James IV. " took in hand the helm of his kingdom " he brought salvation to his people, and evoked the undying spirit of patriotism. The clergy, the nobles and the commonalty were united by a firmer bond than they had hitherto known, and Scotland, acquiring a vast accession of strength morally and materially, began to play an important part in European politics.

Changes, too, were taking place in Edinburgh, the city which old Froissart called the Paris of Scotland, " *car c'est Paris en Ecosse comment que elle ne soit pas France.*" Not long ago it had still been open and undefended. But in the middle of the fifteenth century a new order of things arose, for the citizens were granted " full licence and leiff to fosse, bulwalk, wall, tour, turret and other ways to strength the burgh in quhat maner of dree that be maist spedeful to them " ; and life became more secure. The Palace of Holyrood was completed and encircled by a park of " hares, conies and deare." The nobles settled down in town houses of their own building. Schools were founded so that " their eldest sons and aires should have perfite Latine, with knowledge and understanding of the lawes " ; and in 1507 Walter Chepman and Andro Myller established the first Scottish printing press.

James, who himself spoke six languages, was an admirer and advancer of learned men, and showed them boundless hospitality and friendship. Distinguished foreigners were encouraged at the Court, and finely entertained with " triumphant Tourneys," Jousts and Masques, dancing, minstrelsy and all manner of feasts. Among them rises the honoured shade of Pedro di Ayala, the sharp-witted Spanish Envoy, who, in 1492, paid a memorable visit to the northern capital. His was, indeed, a " fortunate penne." The letters which he wrote to Ferdinand and Isabella are invaluable, describing, as they do, the chivalry, the passions, and the extraordinary talents of this great Mediæval King who managed to " drive all the sciences abreast." For James had a thousand impulses and a thousand moods. He was charitable, and brave, and skilled in all knightly sports. He enjoyed music and dabbled in theology. He loved the mysterious, the unknown, and the fabulous. But his heart's desire was Palestine. He thought perpetually of the Holy Land, and how, when his duties permitted, he would go to the Crusades. As this cherished dream did not materialise, he turned for solace to Alchemy.

It is impossible to exaggerate the importance of Alchemy in the Middle Ages. It was patronised in every country by

Princes and prelates, by lettered and unlettered, all of them
haunted by its illimitable possibilities, and all of them
hoping for miraculous results. Gold was needed. No other
substance under Heaven could compare with it. Gold was
the well-spring of the treasures and riches of this world. . . .
And so they erected their furnaces and alembics, made
singular experiments in transcendental chemistry, and dreamt
of " changing imperfect metal into that which is perfect."
James, wishing to acquire wealth for his fleet, devoted himself with great zeal to this art and incidentally became an
adept at all the curious sciences of the day. He studied the
virtue of herbs and made elixirs. He bought " potingary "
books and gorgeously illuminated alchemistical treatises, but
the latter, despite the magnificent assurances contained in
their titles, proved to be little else than labyrinths of cabalistic
signs. Thus, the secret "which like a rose had been guarded
by thorns, so that few in past times could pull the flower,"
remained unrevealed to him. Quite undaunted, he now
enlarged his sphere by making quaint researches into surgery,
and took as his teacher John Damian, a crafty impostor, who
professed to be a physician. The latter was appointed
Abbot of Tungland, because " he caused the King to believe
that his inventions could make fine gold of other metal,
which science he called the Quintessence, whereupon the
King made great cost but all in vain. This Abbot took in
hand to flie with wingis and laund in Fraunce before the said
Ambassadors, and to that effect he caused make ane pair of
wingis of feathers, which being fastened upon him he flew
off the castel wall of Stirling, but shortly fell to the ground
and brak his thigh bone ; the cause thereof he ascryvit to
that there were sum hen feathers in the wingis which sought
the dunghill, and not the skies." Nor can we blame him for

xi

his credulity, for he lived in an age when all men were credulous.

In James, the Mediæval spirit of chivalry reached its highest expression. It was, with him, a noble passion which unhappily proved his undoing. When Henry VIII. threatened France with invasion, Anne of Brittany dispatched a letter to Scotland with a glove and the ring off her finger, imploring her " Knyght " to advance three feet into English ground to strike a blow in her honour. This prayer was granted without delay. Disregarding all warnings, the King raised a mighty feudal army and led it to its doom. Ten thousand Scotsmen were sacrificed in vain on the fatal field of Flodden. Thus perished James IV. and the flower of his nobility for a quarrel that was none of their making. Well might the Lyon Herald lament in anguish :

> " *I never read in tragedy nor story,*
> *At one journey so many nobles slain*
> *For the defence and love of their sovereign.*" . . .

After the disastrous minority of James V. the Reformation brought fresh actors upon the scene, who " devastated churches throughout all parts of the kingdom ; for everie one made bold to put forth their hands, the meaner sort imitating the example of the greater. The Holy vessels and whatever else men could make gain of, as timber, lead, and bells were put to sale : the very scpulchres of the dead were not spared." The nobility were compelled to humble themselves to a discipline which they hated, and to assume the garb and repeat the Shibboleth of a religion which they did not feel. Inspired by Wishart, John Knox, " who never feared the face of man," swept all before him with his fiery eloquence and implacable severity. Toleration and mercy

were not understood. There was but one Heaven, and one
way to it. A single mass was more to be feared than ten
thousand armed men. . . . So the Presbyterian government
was established on the ruins of the ancient religion, asserting
its right to treat in an ecclesiastical way of greatest and
smallest affairs, from "the King's throne that should be
established in righteousness, to the merchant's balance that
should be used in faithfulness." In 1554 the sacrament of
the Mass was abolished, and Scotland broke for ever with
Rome.

The Reformation had three causes : Papal finance, the
conditions of religious orders, and the publication of the New
Testament. In England it was started by the Crown,
Henry VIII. dethroning the Pope's supremacy and dissolving
both monasteries and convents. In Scotland it was pro-
moted by a knowledge of the scriptures, for the entire nation
turned with indescribable zest to the metrical version of the
Psalms of David, which became the true vernacular poetry
of the day. Thus, a magnificent piece of prose was changed
into doggerel. Sacred themes were now adapted to popular
airs, and "holie songs of veritie" replaced the once "faymed
rhymes of vanity." Although the earliest edition entitled
*The gude and godlie Ballatis* was printed in Edinburgh in
1568, they made their appearance before that date on broad-
sheets which were circulated by wandering minstrels secretly
but swiftly throughout the country. Young and old committed them to memory, and everybody sang them. This
moral and spiritual crisis was not beneficial to literature.
Scholars protested angrily, accusing the versifiers of having
" drunk more of Jordan than of Helicon," and Queen Elizabeth tersely referred to their productions as " Jigs from
Geneva," but despite these criticisms the passion for para-

phrases was universal. Even the Acts of the Apostles were rhymed. And so intense was the spirit of Calvinism, that Alexander Hume, " a godly and painful man," published an exhortation to the youth of Scotland, urging it not only to forswear profane sonnets and vain ballads, but also to lay aside the old romances, and read no other books on love than the Song of Solomon. Wit was wanton. Dancing was not a folly, but a crime. And there was to be no music. . . . This was indeed a singular change.

Meanwhile, at the French Court, Mary Stuart, " *parmy les jeux et les festins*," with subtle-minded and joyous people all about her, and the sound of Ronsard's verses echoing in her ears, was asking for a passport to enable her to return to her native land. And on August 10th, 1561, she landed at Leith. It is neither possible nor necessary to write at length here of her whose charm is " beyond the ruin of time." Perhaps the highest testimony to her power lies in the lines sent by Sir Nicholas White to Secretary Cecil.[1] " She hath an alluring grace, a searching wit clouded with mildness. Then, joy is a lively infective passion, and carries many persuasions to the heart, which ruleth all the rest. And therefore I guess what sight might work in others. But if I might give advice, there should be very few subjects of this land who should have access to, or conference with this lady."

In the sixteenth century there were three distinct sources of inspiration from which Scottish writers could draw. The Bible, the Classics, and local tradition. Records were gradually accumulating. Every country had its heroes and it annals. There was scarcely a mountain, a river, or a forest which did not teem with legends, for Scotland was essentially " the country of the Faerie." The unseen world

[1] *Miscellaneous State Papers* (1501-1720), British Museum.

xiv

was as real as the world of the senses ; and what we now call symbolism was in those days recognised as simple fact. Communion between the cheerful everyday world of the living and the shadowy land beyond the tomb was, it seems, uninterrupted, for dead men's ghosts came harking back on many a sinister errand. The tempest and the mist, too, were peopled with legions of fantastic forms. There were fays and faeries, mandrakes and incubi, hellwains and fire-drakes ; and woe betide the ill-starred traveller who, in a cheerless hour, heard the wild neighing of the Kelpie. Moreover, any event which could not be accounted for, was immediately put down to magic, necromancy, witch-spells or the Devil. There was no compromise ; it was all quite positive. Even the Bible contained injunctions against witches, for instance : " Thou shalt not suffer a witch to live . . ." So, in 1484, when Innocent VIII. lashed out at them in his famous Bull *Summis Desiderantes*, directing that all who practised diabolical arts should be put to death, the result was inevitable. " Wise women " were at once seized, and burned by the hundred, in front of enthralled spectators. Yet it seemed impossible to obliterate them, or to prevent their forbidden rites from being cherished " up and down the country." There were, of course, charms and amulets against the foul fiend and the nightmare. One could sleep crosslegged like the gaunt effigies of the Knights Templars. Churchyard yew and hallowed wax were potent antidotes, and wise parents charged their children to cut twigs off the rowan tree or witchwood to make little crosses which were inserted in the lining of their clothing, as :

> " *Rowan tree and red thread*
> *Keep the witches from their speed* . . ."

But nobody felt secure, and even the most enlightened minds were under the dominion of superstition.

Much of this lore is revealed to us in the Old Ballads. It is reasonable to suppose that the *Canzoni che si cantano ballando* date from about 1400. They were of unknown authorship—which fact did not trouble anybody in those days—and at first seem to have been intended for the unsophisticated taste of the lower classes. The pipers, who were attached to every border town of note, appeared in the spring, and after harvest, to sing their lays to the people who wished for some amusement when the day's work was over. In return for this they were given a night's lodging and a gift of grain. And because their office was hereditary, these men were heirs to a vast store of poetical tradition which had been faithfully kept and elaborated by their fathers. Itinerant musicians, too, playing upon the harp or the primitive fiddle, hawked them about from fair to fair. Everybody loved a song. Everybody loved a story. There were but few pleasures in those days. Books were scarce, and only scholars could read them. Life was very cheerless in the lonely Border Towers. The gates were locked at sunset. It was intolerably cold in the draughty halls, and the smoke stung like nettles. So when the Barons came home from their hawking and hunting and less reputable pursuits, they turned with relief to the minstrels, who tossed them a love-song of ingenuous beauty, or stirred their sluggish minds with tales of " thinges strange and marvellous, like Cloth of Arras opened and put abroad . . ." And we, too, are stirred. There is a starkness in these ballads which reminds us of the old Greek tragedies. They hold something of their restraint and briefness, and disquiet us with the same fear of impending doom. To Addison belongs the honour of having been the first modern writer who revived the ancient Credit of Minstrelsy. In a happy hour, when engaged in a lively war against false wit, he took up the common version of *Chevy Chase*, and lifted it out of the highways into literature. It was an act of great courage. " Had this old song," says he, in *Spectator*, No. 74, " been filled with epigrammatical turns and points of wit, it might perhaps have pleased the wrong taste of some readers, but it would never have become the delight of the common people, nor have warmed the heart of Sir Philip Sidney." He was, one remembers, sharply criticised for his good taste by Dr. Johnson, whose rooted and dogmatic classicism prevented him from seeing any merit in the Border Ballads.

In the seventeenth century little was thought or heard of poetry. The decay of Scots prose also dates from that period. This was inevitable, for the Reformation had done its work well. But when the Royal Family were fugitives in exile they inspired a large number of Jacobite Songs, which form a lasting and sorrowful tribute to the great cause of the Stuarts. These songs have their own magic. They express an unquestioning and touching faith, and bring us face to face with a personal and national loyalty, which has never been surpassed in any country or in any age.

There is a phrase of Horace which might easily apply to the makers of Anthologies, for it defines their limitations. . . . " It is but a poor household that does not contain many valuables unnoted by the master of the house . . ." This little book is but a suggestion, and as such does not pretend to any sort of completeness. The old obligatory items are not included. We can pay our tribute to them elsewhere. I have merely read for my own amusement, and, governed entirely by caprice, have thought it worth while to string together some of the pieces which have given me subtle and peculiar pleasure.

Spelling and punctuation have occasionally been modernised, and speeches condensed, in the interests of simplicity and brevity.

I gratefully acknowledge permission accorded to me by Mr. Bertrand Russell to include some lines of his. My thanks are due to Mrs. Carmichael for kindly allowing me to reprint three poems from the " Carmina Gadelica," and to John Lane, The Bodley Head, Ltd., for an extract from the " Fugger News Letters." And I have to express my gratitude to Lady Dorothea Ruggles-Brise and Sir Charles Cook for valuable advice and to Rev. R. Law for his translation into English of a Latin letter of James IV.

ELEANOR M. BROUGHAM.

LONDON, *October*, 1925.

# PART I

Τὸ ζῆν ἐστιν ὥσπερ οἱ κύβοι·
οὐ ταὔτ' ἀεὶ πίπτουσιν, οὐδὲ τῷ βίῳ
ταὐτὸν διαμένει σχῆμα, μεταβολὰς δ'
ἔχει.                          *Alexis, iv. Cent. B.C.*

Neither our intelligence, nor our beliefs,
Neither our words, nor our deeds,
Neither ourselves, nor our souls ever agree.
    *From " The Divine Songs of Zarathustra."*

Let us then not merely look at the facts, but also carefully
investigate the occasion, the cause, the motive, the difference
of persons, and all the surrounding circumstances. For
only so can we reach the truth.
    *Saint Chrysostom* (347-407).

Tout est dangereux ici-bas, et tout est nécessaire.
    *Voltaire.*

C'est ni le bien-être ni même la liberté qui contribue
beaucoup à l'originalité et à l'énergie du développement
intellectuel ; c'est le milieu des grandes choses, c'est l'activité
universelle, c'est le spectacle des révolutions, cest la passion
développée par le combat.
    *Renan.*

The Past does not change or strive. Like Duncan in
Macbeth " After life's fitful fever it sleeps well ! " What
was eager and grasping, what was petty and transitory has
faded away. The things that were beautiful and eternal
shine out like stars in the night.
    *Bertrand Russell.*

## THE LORD'S PRAYER

Uor fader quhilk beest i' Hevin, Hallowit weird thyne nam. Cum thyne kinrik. Be dune thyne wull as is i' Hevin, sva po yerd. Uor dailie breid gif us thilk day. And forleit us our skaths, as we forleit tham quha skath us. And leed us na intill temtation. Butan fre us fra evil. *Amen*.

## ON THE DEATH OF ALEXANDER III

*This beautiful old lament of a forgotten Makar for Alexander III. (1241-1286), the last of the Celtic kings, quoted in Andrew of Wyntoun's " Orygynale Cronykil of Scotland," c. 1424, is the earliest recorded fragment of Scottish poetry.*

Quhen Alysandyr oure King was dede
That Scotland led in love and le,[1]
Away was sons[2] of ale and brede,
Of wyne and wax of gamyn[3] and gle.

Oure golde was changyd into lede
Christ, borne into Virginité
Succour Scotland and remede
That stands in perplexité.

## THE SIEGE OF EDINBURGH CASTLE (1295)

The Wednesdaie to Edenbrough the abbey, and caused ther to be set iij engyns castyng into the Castell day and nyght; and the Vth daie thei spake of pees. . . .
" *Voyage of Kynge Edwarde into Scotland.*"
*Archœlogia, vol. XXI. p. 478.*

## TWO PROPHECIES OF THOMAS THE RHYMER

*Few personages are so famous in Northern Folk Lore as Thomas of Erceldoune, who flourished in the reign of Alexander III., and was called " the rhymer " on account of his poetical*

[1] Law.    [2] Abundance.
[3] Gambolling.

3

B 2

*romance " Sir Tristrem," which was alluded to by the Trouvères of Normandy and Brittany in the fourteenth century. His prophecies were held in great repute as early as 1306, and in the seventeenth century could still be found in most farm-houses in Scotland. Tradition tells us that he was mysteriously carried off to Elfland, and only after seven years allowed to revisit the earth. The following lines are supposed to be in answer to a question from the heroic Countess of March, known as " Black Agnes," who was renowned for her gallant defence of the Castle of Dunbar against the English in 1339, which incident is told with much detail by Andrew of Wyntoun in his Chronicle. The whole tendency of the prophecy is to aver " that there shall be no end of the Scottish war till a final conquest of the country by England." Sir Walter Scott was of opinion that it was a forgery contrived for the encouragement of the English invaders in the reign of Edward III.*

La Countesse de Donbar demande a Thomas de Essedoune quant la guerre d'Escoce prendreit fyn. E yl l'a repoundy et dyt.

> When man is mad a kyng of a capped man ;
> When man is lever other mones thyng than is owen ;
> [1]When londe thouys forest, ant forest is felde ;
> When hares kendles o' the her'ston ;
> When Wyt and Wille weres togedere :
> When mon makes stables of kyrkes ; and steles castels
>     with styes ;
> When Rokesboroughe nys no burgh ant market is at
>     Forwyleye ;

[1] " When cultivated land shall become forest, and hares litter on the hearthstone."

4

When Bambourne is donged with dede men ;
When men ledes men in ropes to buyen and to sellen ;
[1]When a quarter of whaty whete is chaunged for a colt of
    ten markes ;
When prude (*pride*) prikes and pees is leyd in prisoun ;
When a Scot ne me hym hude ase hare in forme that the
    English ne shall hym fynde ;
When rycht ant wronge astente the togedere ;
When laddes weddeth lovedies (*ladies*) ;
[2]When Scottes flen so faste, that for faute of shep, hy
    drowneth hemselve ;
When shall this be ?
Nouther in thine tyme ne in mine ;
Ah comen ant gone
Withinne twenty winter ant one.

*Pinkerton's Poems, from Maitland's MSS. quoting from
Harl. Lib.* 2253, *F.* 127.

## ON DUNNOTTAR CASTLE

*This sea-beat castle—the Dun Fother of Pictish chronicles—
played a stormy part in the fourteenth century.   It belonged to
the great family of Keith, who filled it with rare treasures.
But it fell from glory in the Jacobite days, became a State
prison, and later a ruin.   Thus the prophecy was fulfilled.*

Dwnnotyr standin by the se,
Lairdless sal thy landis be,
And underneath thy heartstane
The tod (*fox*) sal bring his birdis (*broods*) hame.

----

[1] The exchange between a colt worth ten markes, and a quarter of
" whaty " (*indifferent wheat*) seems to allude to the famine of 1388.
[2] " When Scots flee so fast, that they are drowned for want of ships."

5

## THE DEATH OF SIR GILES DE ARGENTINE AT
## BANNOCKBURN, JUNE 25TH, 1314

*John Barbour (1316-1396), the venerable Archdeacon of Aberdeen, was held in great esteem by Robert II., the first Stuart sovereign. His national epic, " The Bruce," written in octosyllabic rhyme, is valuable for its traditional history of the period 1304-1333, and the far-famed panegyric upon Freedom, which it contains, shows poetical imagery superior to his age. The slaughter of the English at Bannockburn, where Robert Bruce secured the final independence of his kingdom, was immense, and is alluded to with some sarcasm in an old Scottish rhyme preserved in Marlowe's " Edward the Second " :*

> *Maydens of Englande, sore may ye morne*
> *For your lemmans ye have loste at Bannockysborne,*
> > *With heve a lowe.*
> *What, weneth the kynge of Englande*
> *So soone to have wonne Scotlande?*
> > *With rumbylow.*

*Fabian tells us that such songs were sung, accompanied by dances, " in Carolles of ye Maydens and Minstrellys of Scotlande, to the reproofe and dysdane of Englyshmen." These lines refer to Sir Giles de Argentine, a leading Crusader, renowned in the reign of Edward I., who was considered the best Knight in Christendom after Henry of Luxembourg, and the Emperor of Germany.*

> And when Sir Gelis de Argenté
> Saw the king thus and his menie [1]
> Shape them to flee so speedily
> He com richt to the king in hy,[2]

[1] *Menie*, company.          [2] *Hy*, haste.

6

And said " Sir, sen that it is swa [1]
That ye thusgat [2] your gate will ga,
Haifis [3] gude day ! for agane will I ;
Yit fled I never siccarly,
And I cheiss [4] here to bide and die
Than till lif here and shamefully flee."
His bridle than but mair abaid [5]
He turnit, and agane he rade,
And on Sir Edward the Bruce's rout
That was so sturdy and so stout,
As dreid of nakyn thing [6] had he,
He prikit, [7] cryand " Argenté ! "
And they with spearis swa him met,
And swa feill [8] spearis on him set,
That he and horse were chargit swa
That baith doun to the erd can ga ;
And in that place than slain was he.
Of his dede was richt great pitie ;
He was the third best knicht, perfay,
That men wist liffand in his day.

*The Bruce (Book xiii.* 299-322).

## FROM A LETTER OF GEORGE DUNBAR, ELEVENTH EARL OF MARCH TO HENRY IV. (1400)

*In the following letter which is one of the earliest, written in English, the Earl of March complains of the grievous wrong done to him by the brilliant but profligate Duke of Rothesay,*

[1] *Swa,* so.
[2] *Thusgat,* in this gate or manner.
[3] *Haifis,* bid you.
[4] *Cheiss,* choose.
[5] *But mair abaid,* without more delay.
[6] *Nakyn thing,* thing of no kind.
[7] *Prikit,* spurred.
[8] *Feill,* many.

7

*second son of Robert III., who, although married to his daughter,
wished to leave her and " spouse one other wife." He claims
relationship with the English King, and offers to go over to his
side, that he might have his revenge upon his enemies. It must
be remembered that nationality did not exist in those days as we
understand it now.*

EXCELLENT, MYCHTY, AND NOBLE PRINCE.

Like it your Royalty to wit that I am gretly wrangit
by the Duc of Rothesay, the which spousit my douchter, and
now, made by hys letter and his seal, and against the law of
Holy Kirk spouses ane other wife, as it ys said. Of the
which wrang and defowle to me and my douchter in
such manner done, I, as ane of your poor kin, if it
like you, requere you of help for such honest service as I
may do after my power to your noble lordship and to your
land.

Also, noble Prince, will ye deyne to graunt and to send me
your saufcondwyt (*safe conduct*) endurand quhill the feast of
the Nativitie of Seint John the Baptist for a hundred knights
and squires, and servantry, goods, horse, and harnais, as well
within walled town, as without, or in what other reasonable
manere that you like, for travaillyng and dwellyng within
your land.

And, excellent Prince, syn that I clayme to be of kin with
you, and it peradventure nocht knawen on your parte, I
shewe it to your Lordschip by this my lettre, that if Dame
Alice the Bowmount was your gud-dame, Dame Marjory
Comyne, her full sister, was my gud-dame on the tother syde,
sa that I am bot of the feird (*fourth*) degree of kin to you, the
which in olde time was callit neir.

And, noble Prince, marvel ye nocht that I write my lettres

8

in Englishe, fore that ys more clere to myne understandyng than Latyne or Fraunche.

Excellent, mychty and noble Prince, the Haly Trinite hafe you evermare in kepyng.

Writyn at my castell of Dunbarr, the XVIIj day of Feverer.

LE COUNT DE LA MARCHE D'ESCOCE.

Au tresexcellent trespuissant et tresnoble Prince, le Ro Dengleterre.

### ON A FAITHLESS LOVER

*Than* turnis he his sail anon,
    And passes to another port ;
Though she be never so wo-begone,
    Her caris cold are his comfort,
Herefore I pray in termys short,
    Christ keep these *birdis bright in bowers*[1]
*Fra* false lovers, and their resort !
    *Sic* peril lies in paramours !

*Mersar.* (*fl.* 1430).

### GOOD COUNSEL

*James I.* (1394-1437), *one of the wisest of the ill-starred race of Stuarts, " loved letters with incredible warmth, and indulged in singing and piping, in harping and in other honest solaces of grete pleasance and disport." At the age of eleven he embarked for France, but was captured by an English cruiser, and im-*

---

[1] The expression *birdis* (i.e., *brides*) *bright in bowers* was a poetical circumlocution for *women.*

9

*prisoned for eighteen years, chiefly in the Tower of London,
where he learned many accomplishments. In 1423 he was
released, and shortly afterwards returned to Scotland with his
bride, Lady Joanna Beaufort, who was the inspiration of his
great poem " The Kingis Quair," that is, the king's quire or
book, in which he tells us that she had " beauty enough to make
a world to dote." All historians agree that James had a
resolute and lofty character, and ruled wisely and well. A wave
of civilization passed across the country, and " all manner of
virtue spread fast during his time." His tragic death at the
hands of Sir Robert Graham and other conspirators is vividly
described by John Shirley in his " Cronycle of the dethe and
murdure of James Stewarde King of Scotys."*

Sen throw vertew incressis dignitie,
    And vertew is flour and rute of noblesse ay,
Of ony wit, or quhat estait thow be,
    His steppis follow, and dreid for none effray :
    Eject vice, and follow treuth alway :
Lufe maist thy God that first thy lufe began,
And for ilk inche he will the quyte [1] ane span.


Be not ouir proude in they prosperitie,
    For as it commis, sa will it pas away ;
The tyme to compt is schort, thow may weill se,
    For of grene gress sone cummis wallowit [2] hay.
    Labour in treuth, quhilk suith is of thy fay ; [3]
Traist maist in God, for he best gyde the can,
And for ilk inche he will the quyte ane span.


[1] Requite.                  [2] Withered.
[3] Which is the truth (substance) of thy faith.

Sen word is thrall, and thocht is only fre,
 Thou dant [1] thy toung, that power hes and may,[2]
Thou steik [3] thy ene fra warldis vanite :
 Refraine thy lust, and harkin quhat I say :
  Graip or [4] thow slyde, and keip furth [5] the hie-way,
Thou hald the fast upon thy God and man,
And for ilk inche he will the quyte ane span.

QUOD KING JAMES THE FIRST
*From " The Gude and Godlie Ballates," 1578.*

MORALITAS FROM ''THE TAILL OF THE
UPLANDIS MOUS.''

*Robert Henryson (c. 1430-1506), said to have been a school
master of Dunfermline, was the writer of the earliest Scottish
pastoral " Robene and Makyne " but his most appealing work
is the " Testament of Cresseid," a lovely tale of passion and
of pity, in which the [6] rhyme royal is used with tragic effect. It
was inspired by Chaucer's " Troilus and Creseide," and Sir
Francis Kynaston translated it into Latin verse in the time of
Charles I. Henryson's metrical version of thirteen " Morall
Fabillis of Esope," written " by request and precept of a lord,
of whom the name it needs not record," printed in 1570,
casts a good deal of light upon the manners and customs of the
day ; and is vigorous and full of humour, with a marked
flavour of realism.*

Blissit be sempill lyfe withoutin dreid !
 Blissit be sober feist in quyetie !
Quha hes aneuch, of na mair hes he neid,
 Thocht it be lytill in-to quantitie.

[1] Tame thou.     [2] Is mighty.        [3] Close thou.
     [4] Grope ere.        [5] Forward.
     [6] Owes its name to the King's Quair.

Greit abondance and blind prosperitie
Oftymes makis ane evill conclusioun.
The sweitest lyfe thairfor in this cuntrie
Is sickernes,[1] with small possessioun.

O wantoun man, that usis for to feid
  Thy wambe,[2] and makis it ane god to be,
Luik to thy-self ! I warne thee wele, but dreid :
  The cat cummis and to the mous hes ee.
  Quhat vaillis than thy feist and rialtie,
  With dreidful hart and tribulacioun ?
  Thairfoir best thing in eird, I say, for me,
Is blyithnes in hart, with small possessioun.

Thy awin fyre, my friend, sa it be bot ane gleid,[3]
  It warmis weill, and is worth gold to thee ;
And Solomon sayis, gif that thow will reid,
  " Under the hevin it can nocht better be
  Than ay be blyith and leif in honestie."
Quhairfoir I may conclude be this ressoun,
  Of eirthly joy it beiris maist degrie,
Blyithnes in hart, with small possessioun.


EPITAPH OF CRESSEID

Lo, fair ladies, Cresseid of Troy's towne,
Sometime counted the flour of womenheid,
Under this stane, late leper, lieth deid.

From the Testament of Cresseid.

[1] Security.                    [2] Stomach.
          [3] A tiny flame.

12

## THE PRAIS OF AGE

Into ane garth, under ane reid roseir,
　　Ane auld man, and decrepit, heard I syng ;
Gay was the note, sweit was the voice and cleyr ;
　　It was grit joy to heir of sic ane thyng.
　　" And to my doume," he said, in his dytyng,
" For to be young I wald nocht, for my wyss,
　　Of all this world to mak me lord and king :
The moyr [1] of aige the nerar hevynis bliss.


" Fals is this warld, and full of varyance,
　　Oureset with syt[2] and uther synnys mo ;
Now trewth is tynt,[3] gyle hes the governance,
　　And wrachitness hes wrocht al weill to wo ;
　　Fredoume is tynt, and flemyt[4] the lordis fro,
And cuvattyce is all the cause of this :
　　I am content that yowthheid is ago [5] :
The moyr of aige the nerar hevynis blis.


" The stait of yowth I repute for na gude,
　　For in that stait grit perrell now I se ;
Can nane gane-stand the rageing of his blude
　　Na yit be stabil quhill that he aigit be :
　　Than of the thing that maist rejoysit he,
Na-thing remaynis for to be callit his ;
　　For quhy ? it was bot verray vanite :
The moyr of aige the nerar hevynis blyss.


[1] More.　　　　　[2] Grief.　　　　　[3] Lost.
[4] Driven away.　　　　　　　　　　　[5] Gone.

13

" This wrechit warld may nay man trowl [1]; for quhy ?
  Of erdly joy ay sorrow is the end ;
The gloyr of it can na man certify,
  This day a king, the morne na-thing to spend !
  Quhat haif we heyr bot grace us to defend !
The quhilk God grant us till amend our myss,[2]
  That till his joy he may our saullis send ;
The moyr of aige the nerar hevynis bliss."

*Idem.*

## TWEED AND TILL

*The Tweed is a broad, clear and rapid river, provided with fords, but its tributary, the Till, is narrow, deep and slow. The greater danger of the Till is expressed in the following lines :*

Tweed says to Till,
" What gars ye rin sae still ? "
Till says to Tweed,
" Though ye rin wi' speed,
And I rin slaw,
Yet where ye droun ae man,
I droun twa ! "

## EDINBURGH

*This sinister malediction refers to the murder of William, Earl of Douglas, who was basely killed in Edinburgh Castle in 1440. While he was dining, a bull's head, the signal of death, was brought in. He was instantly subjected to a mock trial, and beheaded " in the back court of the Castle that lieth to the*

---

[1] Trust.        [2] Fault.

*west."  The following is unfortunately the only stanza pre-
served to us of an ancient ballad, given by Hume of Godscroft,
dealing with this tragic story :*

> Edinburgh castle, town, and tower,
> God grant thou sink for sinne,
> And that even for the black dinoure
> Erle Douglas gat therein.

## FROM THE RECORDS OF THE CITY OF ABERDEEN

In the year 1482, no man was to open his booth on the
Sabbath Day under the pain of a pound of wax to St.
Nicholas.

In the year 1493, Robert Walker was fined eight pennies
for putting away the water from the spout of the preaching
friars of St. John.

In the year 1498 the town grants to Magnus Cobben
twenty pennies to buy a coat, to pass ilk morning of ilk
Monday through the town, to name and pray for their souls,
giving him a bell as use is, and has been in times past.

In the year 1507, William Hay, Chaplain to our Lady
Chapel at the Bridge of Dee, delivered to the magistrates one
chain of silver, one image of silver of our lady, both over-gilt,
three napkins, an altar towel, together with the keys of the
altar.

The same year, June the 12th, the barbers were admitted
into a free craft, and all the privileges that other crafts
have.

15

## O DOUGLAS, O DOUGLAS, TENDER AND TRUE

*When Robert Bruce, hero of the Scottish War of Independence, died of leprosy in 1329, the good Lord James of Douglas enclosed his heart in a silver casket, according to his promise to the dead King ; and, accompanied by a hundred loyal Knights, set out upon a pious pilgrimage to the Holy Land, there to bury it. But in Spain he was attacked by the Saracens and perished before the spears of Alonzo of Castile could come to his assistance. As he was dying, he threw the jewelled case containing the sacred relic among the Infidels, for the actual command given him by Bruce had been to carry it " against the enemies of God." . . . Thus fell Lord James above the heart of his King, and the ancient prophecy " that after death it should pass once more in fiery fight against the foe " was fulfilled. It was rescued by Logan and Lockhart and brought back to Melrose Abbey. These stirring lines, written by a partisan of the House of Douglas, describe the incident.*

Amang the heathen men, the hart hardely he slang,
Said, " Wend on as Thou was wont,
   Thro the battell in front.
   Aye formost in the front,
   Thy foes among."

           *From the " Buke of the Howlat," by*
           *Richard Holland (fl. 1450).*

## THE DEATH OF THE BRUCE

I will that as soone as I am trepassed out of this worlde that ye take my harte owte of my body, and embawme it, and take of my treasoure as ye shall thynke sufficient for that entreprise, both for your selfe and suche company as ye wyll

16

take with you, and present my hart to the holy Sepulchre where as our Lorde laye, seyng my body can nat come there. And take with you suche company and purueyaunce as shalbe aparteynyng to your estate. And where soeuer ye come let it be knowen howe ye cary with you the harte of kyng *Robert* of *Scotland*, at his instaunce and desire, to be presented to the holy Sepulchre. Than all the lordes that herde these wordes, wept for pitie. And whan this knyght, syr *William Duglas* myght speke for wepyng, he sayd : A, gentle & noble kyng, a .C. tymes I thanke your grace of the great honour that ye do to me, sith of so noble and great treasure ye gyve me in charge. And syr I shall do with a glad harte all that ye haue commaunded me, to the best of my true power, howe be it I am nat worthy nor sufficient to achyve suche a noble entreprise. Than the kyng sayd, A, gentle knyght, I thanke you so that ye wyl promyse to do it. Sir, sayd the knyght, I shall do it vndoubtedly, by the faythe that I owe to God, and to the ordre of knyghthode. Than I thanke you, sayd the kyng : for nowe shall I dye in more ease of my mynde, sith that I knowe that the most worthy and sufficient knyght of my realme shall achyue for me, the whiche I coulde neuer atteyne unto. And thus soone after thys noble *Robert de Bruse* kyng of *Scotland*, trepassed out of this uncertain world in the year of our Lord God M.CCC. XXVII. the VII. day of the Moneth of Novembre.

*From Froissart's Chronicles, translated by John Bourchier, Lord Berners* (1467–1533).

AN ANCIENT CURSE

*The traditionary tale of " The lands of Forvee " is that early in the fifteenth century the Laird to whom the parish belonged died, leaving his lands to his three beautiful daughters. These helpless orphans were despoiled of their inheritance, and in the bitterness of their spirit prayed Heaven to make the fair fields of which they had been defrauded worthless to the ravager and his posterity. Their prayer was heard. A furious storm arose, and the parish was wholly overblown with sand.*

> Yf ever maydens malysone [1]
> Dyd licht upon drye lande ;
> Let nochte bee found in Furvye's glebys
> But thystle, bente,[2] and sande.

## LETTER FROM EDWARD IV. TO JAMES III., KING OF SCOTS, 1461

*This letter was written after the battle of Towton, near York, when Henry VI. had surrendered Berwick to the Scots to obtain their help.*

Edward, by the grace of God, King of England and of France, to our dear cousin, James, by the same grace, King of Scots, greeting. Whereas ye took and received unto your land our traitors and rebels, Henry, late usurpant king of our said realm,[3] Margaret his wife, Edward her son, and other our traitors and rebels, not become your liegemen yet ; omitting thereby the duty of the state and worship that ye be of, should bear to the noble princehood, we exhort and require you, in God's behalf, to deliver unto us without delay

---

[1] Malediction.   [2] Dry grass.
[3] The strongminded Margaret of Anjou, who, owing to the weak intellect of the King, was the virtual sovereign. After her defeat at Towton, where she bravely led the Lancastrian troops, she placed her young son (who was slain at Tewkesbury in 1471) in the keeping of the Bishop of Saint Andrews, and determined to intrigue with the Scots against Edward.

our said traitors and rebels, if they become not your lieges and subjects ; and if it so be, to certify us the same under seal ; showing yourself unto us in these, as in like case ye would we or any other prince should show them to you.

*Harl.* 543, *f.* 148.

## HOW THE GOOD KNIGHT REASONED WITH HIS SON

This good Knight reasoned with his son in this manner, as follows : saying, my dear and best beloved son, when I behold and consider thy great beauty and strength, seemliness of person, thy manhood, and well doing in arms, it gives me to great consolation and blytheness in my heart, for above all things earthly, next my own proper flesh, I love thee ; but when I remember and consider the great abuse and folly that thou uses in the delectation and pleasure that thou hast in women, which thou callest love, I take there in so great thoughts and melancholy, that it will never drive the life out of my feeble body : Therefore, my dearly beloved son, I require and admonish thee, through the obedience and love that thou owe to thy father, that thou attend and incline thy heart to it as I shall say, for I shall explain and interpret to thee many great evils and misfortunes that has come, and daily comes, to men, through that foul delectation of women, which thou callest love ; and for what cause it should be eschewed and the dictes or sayings of the holy fathers and wise philosophers.

My son, it is oft times read, how our first father Adam was put from the bliss of Paradise for the breaking of the precepts of God, through the counsel and inducing of our mother Eve. It is written in the Bible how Judith, the woman, cut

19                                                            C 2

off Holophernes' head, while he slept in his pavilion. What was cause of the great wars of Troy ? where so many noble kings, princes, knights and men of good were slain. Hector and all the nobles on both the sides were destroyed, and put down ; the noble city and palace of Ilion burnt and turned into wilderness. Or how quit Cresseid her true lover Troilous, and forgot his long service in love, when she forsook him for Dyomid ; and thereafter went common among the Greeks, and died in great misery and pain !

Oh ! how many realms and towns, kings, princes and noble men, have been destroyed and put down through the wickedness of evil women ! Therefore, my dear son, as thou wilt have my blessing, imprint the saws of these holy and wise men in thy mind, and let their royal examples be a mirror unto thee, to the end that thou fall not in such evil adventures, that is, before written.

*Translated from the Latin in the City of St. Andrews, in July, 1492, by " ane clerk who had been into Venus' Court for the space of more than twenty years."*

## THOMAS OF ERCELDOUNE

'Ο 'Ηράκλειτός φησι, τοῖς ἐγρηγορόσιν ἕνα καὶ κοινὸν κόσμον εἶναι, τῶν δὲ κοιμωμένων ἕκαστον εἰς ἴδιον ἀποστρέφεσθαι.

*Plutarch, De Superstitione.*

*This old song breathes an unconscious beauty which disarms all criticism, and in it there is more than a strain of magic. We are stirred by the dramatic contrast of the ingenuous happiness of Thomas, to whom seven years in the uncertain twilight of Elfland had been as three days, and the utter weariness of the strange and marvellous Faery Queen who, because she loved him, restored him to this world, lest he should be chosen for the tribute paid to Hell.*

*It seems that the story is another version of the Chanson de Geste of Ogier le Danois, written by Raimbert of Paris before 1150.*

Als I me went this endres day,
  Full fast in mynd makand my mone,
In a mery mornyng of May,
  By Huntlee bankes myself allone,

I herd the jay and the throstell;
  The mavys menyde hir in hir song;
The wodewale beryde as a bell,
  That all the wode abowt me rong.

Allone in longyng als I lay,
  Undyrnethe a semely tree,
Saw I whare a lady gay
  Came riding over a lufly lee. . . .

Hir palfray was a dappill-gray—
  Such one ne saw I never none.
As dose the sonne on someres day,
  That faire lady hirself she schone.

Hir selle [1] it was of roell bone [2]—
  Semely was that syght to see!—
Stifly sett with precyous stone,
  And compast all with crapotee,

With stones of Oryent, grete plente.
  Hir hair abowt hir hede it hang.
She rade over that lufly lee;
  A whyl she blew, another she sang.

[1] Saddle.                    [2] Ivory.

Hir garthes of nobyll sylk thay were,
The bukylls were of berel stone,
Hir sterraps werc of crystal clere,
And all with perel over bygone.

Hir payetrel [1] was of irale fyne ;
Hir cropour was of orpharë ;
Hir brydill was of golde fyne—
One aythir syde hang bellys three. . . .

Thomas rathely [2] up he rase,
And ran over that mountayn hye ;
If it be als the story says,
He hir mette at Eldon tree.[3]

He knelyde down appon his knee,
Undirnethe that grenwode spray :
" Lufly lady, rewe on me,
Qwene of heven, as thou wel may ! "

Than spake that lady milde of thoght :
" Thomas, let such wordes be !
Qwene of heven ne am I noght,
For I tuke never so high degre ;

But I am of another countree,
If I be payreld most of pryse.
I ryde aftyr this wylde fee ;
My raches rynnys at my devyse." . . .

" Lufly lady, rewe on mee,
And I will evermore with thee dwell,
Here my troth I plyght to thee,
Whethir thou will in heven or helle."

[1] Horse's breastplate.                    [2] Quickly.
[3] Eildon tree was at the foot of the Eildon hills, above Melrose.

22

" Man of molde, thou will me merre,[1]
    Bot yit thou sall hafe all thy will ;
Bot trowe thou wele, thou chevys the werre,[2]
    For alle my beaute thou will spyll."

Down than lyghte that lady bryght,
    Undirnethe that grenewode spray ;
And, als the story tellis full ryght,
    Seven years by hir he lay. . . .

Thomas stod up in that stede,
    And he byheld that lady gay :
Hir hair it hang all over hir hede,
    Hir ene semede out, that were so gray.

And all the rich clothyng was away,
    That he byfore saw in that stede ;
Hir a schanke black, hir other gray,[3]
    And all hir body lyke the lede.

Than said Thomas : " Allas, allas !
    In fayth, this es a doleful syght !
How art thou faded in the face,
    That shon byfore als the sonne so bright."

Sche sayd : " Thomas, take leve of sonne and mone,
    And of the leaves that grows on tree ;
This twelmonth sall thou with me gone,
    And medill-erthe sall thou not see."

" Allas," he sayd, " and wo is mee !
    I trowe my dedis wyll wirk me care.
My saule, Jesu, byteche [4] I the,
    Whensoever my bones sall fare."

[1] Ruin.                     [2] Thrives the worse.
[3] One leg black, the other grey.    [4] Commit.

She ledde hym in at Eldone Hill,
  Undirnethe a derne [1] lee,
Whare it was dark als mydnyght myrk,
  And ever the water till his knee.

The montenans [2] of dayes three,
  He herd bot swoghying [3] of the flode ;
At the laste he sayd : " Full wo is mee !
  Almast I dye for fault of fode."

She led hym intill a faire herbere,
  Whare frute was growand gret plentee ;
Pere and appill both rype thay were,
  The date, and als the damasee.

The fygge, and also the wyneberye ;
  The nyghtgales byggande [4] on thair nest,
The popinjays fast abowt gan flye,
  And throstylls sang, wolde hafe no rest.

He pressede to pull frute with his hand,
  Als man for food that was nere faynt.
She sayd : " Thomas, thou let them stand,
  Or ells the fiend the will atteynt.

If thou it pluck, sothely to say,
  Thi saule gose to the fyre of helle ;
It commes never out at Domesday,
  But ther in payne ay for to duelle."

" *Seest thou now yon faire way,*
  *That lies over yon hegh mountayn ?*
*Yon is the waye to heven for ay,*
  *When synfull sawles are passed ther payn.*

[1] Secret.  [2] Period.
[3] Roaring.  [4] Building.

24

*Seest thou now yon other way,*
  *That lies lawe bynethe yon ryse?*
*Yon es the way, the sothe to say,*
  *Unto the joye of Paradyse.*

*Seese thou yitt yon thirde way,*
  *That lies undir yon grene plain?*
*Yon is the way, with tears and tray*
  *Whare synfull saulis suffirris thair payn.*

*Bot seese thou now yone ferthe way,*
  *That lygges over yon depe delle?*
*Yon is the way—so waylaway!—*
  *Unto the burning fyr of helle.*

Seese thou yitt yon faire castell,
  That standis over yon highe hill?
Of towne and towre it beris the bell;
  In erthe es none lyke thertill." . . .

" When thou commes to yon castell gay,
  I pray thee curtase man to bee;
And whatso any man to thee say,
  Luke thou answere none bot mee . . . "

Thomas dwelled in that solace
  More than I yow saye, parde,
Till on a day—so hafe I grace!—
  My lufly lady sayd to mee :

" Buske ¹ thee, Thomas, thee buse agayn,
  For here thou may no lengar be;
Hye thee faste with myght and mayn;
  I sall thee bryng till Eldone tree."

¹ Prepare.

25

Thomas sayd than with hevy chere :
" Lufly lady, now let me bee,
For certaynly I hafe benc here
    Noght bot the space of dayes three."

" Forsothe, Thomas, als I thee tell,
    Thou hast bene here thre yere and more,
And langer here thou may not duell ;
    The skyll I sall thee tell wharefore :

To-morne of helle the foule fende
    Amang this folk will fetch his fee ;
And thou art mekill man and hende—
    I trow full wele he wil chose thee.

For all the gold that ever may bee
    Fro hence unto the worldis ende,
Thou bese never betrayed for mee ;
    Therefore with me I rede thou wende."

She broght hym agayn to Eldone tree,
    Undirnethe that grenewode spray.—
In Huntlee bankes es mery to bee,
    Where fowles synges both nyght and day.

                                        *Thornton MS.*

THE CHARACTER OF JAMES IV. DESCRIBED IN
A LETTER FROM PEDRO DI AYALA TO FERDINAND
AND ISABELLA OF SPAIN (JULY 25TH, 1498)

*Pedro di Ayala, Spanish Ambassador to Scotland, was an
intimate friend of James IV.   Although he was also accredited
to the Court of England, he both understood and liked Scotland
better.   Possessed of a keen intelligence, his contemporary*

*accounts are of untold value. They express boundless admiration for the King's wisdom and virtues. Erasmus, too, testifies to the latter's " wonderful force of intellect, and astounding knowledge of everything." James exerted himself to reduce his kingdom to peace and unity, and " everie man loved his prince so well that they would in no ways disobey him." Thus the proud title, " Greatest of the Stuarts," was not undeserved.*

The King is 25 years and some months old. He is of noble stature, neither tall nor short, and as handsome in complexion and shape as a man can be. His address is very agreeable. He speaks the following foreign languages : Latin, very well ; French, German, Flemish, Italian, and Spanish ; Spanish as well as the Marquis, but he pronounces it more distinctly. His own Scottish language is as different from English as Aragonese from Castilian. The King speaks, besides, the language of the savages who live in some parts of Scotland and on the islands. It is as different from Scottish as Biscayan is from Castilian. His knowledge of languages is wonderful. He is well read in the Bible and in some other devout books. He is a good historian. He has read many Latin and French histories, and has profited by them, as he has a very good memory. He never cuts his hair or his beard. It becomes him very well. He fears God and observes all the precepts of the Church. He does not eat meat on Wednesdays and Fridays. He would not ride on Sundays for any consideration, not even to mass. He says all his prayers. Before transacting any business he hears two masses. After mass he has a cantata sung, during which he sometimes despatches very urgent business. He gives alms liberally ; but is a severe judge, especially in the case of murderers. He has a great predilection for priests, and receives advice from them, especially from the Friars Observant, with whom he confesses.

Rarely, even in joking, a word escapes him that is not the truth. He prides himself much upon it, and says it does not seem to him well for kings to swear their treaties as they do now. The oath of a king should be his royal word, as was the case in bygone days. He is neither prodigal nor avaricious, but liberal when occasion requires. He is courageous, even more so than a king should be. I am a good witness of it. I have seen him often undertake most dangerous things in the last wars. On such occasions he does not take the least care of himself. He is not a good captain, because he begins to fight before he has given his orders. He said to me that his subjects serve him with their persons and goods, in just and unjust quarrels, exactly as he likes, and that therefore he does not think it right to begin any warlike undertaking without being himself the first in danger. His deeds are as good as his words. For this reason and because he is a very humane prince, he is much loved. He is active, and works hard.

When he is not at war he hunts in the mountains. I tell your Highnesses the truth when I say that God has worked a miracle in him, for I have never seen a man so temperate in eating and drinking out of Spain. Indeed, such a thing seems to be superhuman in these countries. He lends a willing ear to his counsellers, and decides nothing without asking them ; but in great matters he acts according to his own judgment, and, in my opinion, he generally makes a right decision. I recognise him perfectly in the conclusion of the last peace, which was made against the wishes of the majority in his kingdom.

When he was a minor he was instigated by those who held

the government to do some dishonourable things. They favoured his love intrigues with their relatives, in order to keep him in their subjection. As soon as he came of age, and understood his duties, he gave up these intrigues. When I arrived, he was keeping a lady [1] with great state in a castle. . . Afterwards he sent her to the house of her father, who is a knight, and married her. He did the same with another lady,[2] by whom he had had a son. It may be about a year since he gave up, so at least it is believed, his love-making, as well from fear of God, as from fear of scandal in this world, which is thought very much of here. I can say with truth that he esteems himself as much as though he were Lord of the world. He loves war so much that I fear, judging by the provocation he receives, the peace will not last long. War is profitable to him and to the country.

*B.M. Spanish Calenders* 1, *No.* 210.

### BULL OF POPE ALEXANDER VI

*Alexander VI. (Roderigo Borgia) confirmed the foundation of the University of Aberdeen in 1495. It was called King's College in honour of James IV., who took a keen interest in its establishment.*

. . . Because in the northerly parts of the kingdom there are some places separated from the rest of the realm by arms of the sea and very steep mountains, in which regions dwell men who are uncultivated, and ignorant of letters and almost wild, who on account of the too great distance from seats of

---

[1] Probably Margaret Drummond (1472–1501), who resided at Stirling Castle under the care of Lady Lundy, bore the King a daughter, and was eventually poisoned.
[2] Margaret Boyd, mother of the brilliant Alexander Stuart (1495–1513), Archbishop of St. Andrews, who perished at Flodden Field.

learning and the dangers of travelling thither are not able to devote themselves to letters, nay, are so ignorant of them, that, not only for preaching the word of God to the people of these parts, but also for the ministration of the church ordinances, fit men are not to be found . . . and as King James eagerly desires that in the city of old Aberdeen and in the northern islands and mountains aforesaid, in which there is a healthy climate and abundance of the necessaries of life and suitable dwellings, there be erected and established a university, wherefore the king hath caused us to be humbly petitioned . . . that there be henceforth, to flourish in all time coming, a university of general study, as well in theology and canon and civil law, and medicine and the liberal arts, as in every other lawful faculty, in which, as at Paris and Bologna and any other universities so privileged, all churchmen holding whatever ecclesiastical office, and laymen, masters and doctors, may teach, and at which those desirous to learn, whencesoever they may come, may study and profit. . . . . We therefore, &c.

*Nat. MSS. Scot.*

## ADVICE TO LEESOME [1] MERRINESS

When I have done consider
This warldis vanitie,
Sa brukil and sa slidder,[2]
Sa full of miserie ;
Then I remember me
That here there is no rest ;
Therefore apparentlie
To be merrie is best.

[1] Lawful.                    [2] Brittle and slippery.

Let us be blyth and glad,
My friendis all, I pray.
To be pensive and sad
Na-thing it help us may.
Therefore put quite away
All heaviness of thocht :
Thoch we murne nicht and day
It will avail us nocht.

*Sir Richard Maitland* (1496–1586).

## WAR SUMMONS THE LOVER

Now leif thy mirth, now leif thy haill plesance ;
Now leif thy bliss, now leif thy childis age ;
Now leif thy youth, now follow thy hard chance ;
Now leif thy lust, now leif thy marrïage ;
Now leif thy lufe, for thou sall loss a gage
Whilk never in erd sall be redeemit again ;
    Follow Fortoun, and all her fierce outrage ;
    Go lif in weir, go lif in cruel pain.

Fy on Fortoun, fy on thy frewall [1] wheel ;
Fy on thy traist, for here it has no lest ;
Thou transfigurit Wallace out of his weal,
When he traistit for till haif lestit best.
His plesance here till him was bot a gest ;
Throw thy fierce course, that has na hap to ho, [2]
    Him thou ourthrew out of his likand rest,
    Fra great plesance, in weir, [3] travail, and woe.

*Henry the Minstrel* (1460–1492).

[1] Fickle.                                          [2] Stop.

[3] Debt.

31

## TO THE PRINCESS MARGARET
## ON HER ARRIVAL AT HOLYROOD (1503)

*William Dunbar (c. 1460–1530), the crafty Franciscan poet who had tramped and begged in England, stands supreme in Scotland without equal or second. He enjoyed high favour at the Court of James IV., chronicled many of the events of his reign with liveliness and vivacity, and in the following lines immortalised the King's marriage to Margaret Tudor, the headstrong daughter of Henry VII. This alliance ultimately led to the union of the crowns.*

Now fair, fairest of every fair,
Princess most pleasant and preclare,
The lustiest one alive that been,
   Welcome of Scotland to be Queen !

Young tender plant of pulcritude,
Descended of Imperial blood ;
Fresh fragrant flour of fair-heid sheen,[1]
   Welcome of Scotland to be Queen !

Sweet lusty luesome [2] lady clear,
Most mighty kinges dochter dear,
Born of a princess most serene,
   Welcome of Scotland to be Queen !

Welcome the Rose both red and white,
Welcome the flour of our delight !
Our secret rejoicing from the sun bien,[3]
   Welcome of Scotland to be Queen ;
   Welcome of Scotland to be Queen !

[1] *Fair-heid sheen*, beauty bright.      [2] *Luesome*, worthy of love.
[3] *Bien*, warm.

32

## THE LADY MARGARET IS CONVEYED INTO SCOTLAND

All this Wynter was preparations made for the conveyance of the Ladye Margaret, affianced to the King of Scottes into Scotland. And when all things were readie, the King removed the last day of June from Rychemond, having in his company his sayde daughter and came to Colyweston, where the Countess of Richmond his mother then lay. And after certayne days of solace ended, the King gave her his blessing with a fatherly exhortation and committed the conveyance of her to the King her husband's presence to the Erle of Surrey : and the Erle of Northumberlande was appointed as Wardeyn of the Marches to delyver her at the Confines of both the Marches. Thus this fayre Ladie was conveyed with a great company of Lordes, Ladies, Knightes, Esquires and Gentlemen, till shee cane to Berwick and from thence to a Village called Lambeton Kyrke in Scotland, where the King with the floure of Scotland was readie to receave her, to whom the Erle of Northumberland, according to his commission delyvered her. The Scottes that day, I assure you were not behind the Englishmen, but farre above, both in apparell and riche jewels and massy Chaynes : But above all other the Erle of Northumberland, what with the ryches of his Cote being Goldsmiths worke, garnished with pearle and stone, and what for the costly apparell of the Henxmen and galant trappings of their horses, besides foure hundred tall men, well horsed and appareled in his colours, that he was esteemed both of the Scottes and Englishmen more lyke a prince than a subject. Then was this Ladie conveyed to the town of Edenborough, and there the day after, King James IV. in the presence of all his nobilitie espoused the sayde fayre

Princesse, and feasted the English Lordes, and shewed to them Joustes and other pastimes, very honourably, after the fashion of his rude Countrey. When all things were done and furnished according to their commission, the Erle of Surrey with all the Englishe Lords and Laydes returned into their Countrie, giving more prayse to the manhood, and to the good manner and nurture of Scotlande.

*From Grafton's Chronicle,* 1569.

## THE MEETING OF JAMES IV. AND MARGARET, AUGUST, 1503

*The marriage of James IV. is said to have been one of the most gorgeous spectacles ever witnessed in Edinburgh. He met his bride at Liberton, where she left her litter and mounted on a palfrey behind the King. They were welcomed by pageants and processions, and the Black Friars presented them with a phial containing " three drops of the blood of Christ."*

The King was conveyed to the Queen's chamber, where she met him at her great chamber door, right honourably accompanied. At the meeting he and she made great reverences the one to the other, his head being bare ; and they kissed together, and in like wise kissed the ladies, and others also. And he in especial welcomed the earl of Surrey very heartily.

Then the Queen and he went aside and communed together by long space. She held good manner, and he bareheaded during the time ; and many courtesies passed. Incontinent was the board set and served. They washed their hands in humble reverences ; and after set them down together, where many good devices were rehearsed.

After the supper they washed again, with the reverences ;

34

minstrels began to blow, whereupon danced the Queen, accompanied of my lady of Surrey. This done, the King took leave of her, for it was late ; and he went to his bed at Edinburgh, very well content of so fair meeting, and that he had found the fair company together. . . .

Next day at four of the clock, after dinner, the archbishops of York and of Glasgow and others went to meet the King, but the King, flying as the bird seeks her prey, took another way, and came privily to the said castle, and entered within the chamber with a small company, where he found the Queen playing at cards. . . . In communing together, came the same lords ; to whom the King did reverence. . After some words rehearsed betwixt them, the minstrels began to play a bass dance, the which was danced by the said Queen and the Countess of Surrey. . Incontinent the King began before her to play on the claricords,[1] and after on the lute, which pleased her very much, and she had great pleasure to hear him. . . . The King took leave of her and went to his horse, on whom he did leap without putting the foot within the stirrup. And the said horse was a right fair courser ; and incontinent the King spurred, followed who might.  *John Young, Somerset Herald.*

A NEW YEAR'S GIFT TO KING JAMES IV.

My prince in God gife thee guid grace,
Joy, glaidness, comfort, and solace,
Play, pleasance, mirth, and merrie cheer,
In hansel of [2] this guid new year.

[1] James IV. was a great lover of music, and carried his instruments about with him from place to place. A Moorish " taubronar clad in blak and rede " was established at Court, and four Italian minstrels formed part of the household.

[2] *In hansel of*, as a beginning gift to.

God gife to thee ane blissed chance,
And of all virtue abundance,
And grace ay for to persevere,
    In hansel of this guid new year.

God gife thee guid prosperitie,
Fair fortoun and felicitie,
Evermair in earth while thou are here,
    In hansel of this guid new year.

The heavenlie Lord his help thee send,
Thy realm to rule and to defend,
In peace and justice it to steer,
    In hansel of this guid new year.

God gife thee bliss wherever thou bounes,[1]
And send thee many Fraunce crounes,
Hie liberal heart, and handis nocht sweir[2]
    In hansel of this guid new year
                                *William Dunbar.*

## MARGARET OF SCOTLAND TO
## HENRY VII. (1503)

*The young Queen of Scotland was about fourteen years old
when she wrote this letter.*

My most dear lord and father, in the most humble wise
that I can think I recommend me unto your Grace beseeching
you of your daily blessing, and that it will please you to give
hearty thanks to all your servants, the which by your commandment have given right good attendance on me at this
time, and specially to all these ladies and gentlewomen which

---

[1] *Bounes*, makest ready, preparest to go.
[2] *Sweir*, lazy, illiberal.

hath accompanied me hither, and to give credence to this good lady the bearer hereof, for I have showed her more of my mind than I will write at this time. Sir, I beseech your Grace to be good and gracious lord to Thomas, which was footman to the Queen my mother, whose soul God have assoyle ; for he hath been one of my footmen hither with as great diligence and labour, to his great charge, of his own good and true mind. I am not able to recompense him, except the favour of your Grace. Sir, as for news I have none to send, but that my lord of Surrey [1] is in great favour with the King here that he cannot forbear the company of him no time of the day. He and the bishop of Moray [2] ordereth everything as nigh as they can to the King's pleasure. I pray God it may be for my poor heart's ease in time to come. They call not my Chamberlain to them, which I am sure will speak better for my part than any of them that be of that council. And if he speak anything for my cause, my lord of Surrey hath such words unto him that he dare speak no further. God send me comfort to His pleasure, and that I and mine that be left here with me be well entreated such ways as they have taken. For God's sake, Sir, hold me excused that I write not my self to your Grace, for I have no leisure this time, but hold a wish I would I were with your Grace now, and many times more, when I would answer. As for this that I have written to your Grace, it is very true, but I pray God I may find it well for my welfare hereafter. No more to your Grace at this time, but our Lord have you in his keeping. Written with the hand of your humble daughter,

MARGARET.

[1] Who later slew James IV. at Flodden.
[2] Andrew Forman, a papal pro-notary, who played a conspicuous part in European diplomacy.

## LETTER FROM JAMES IV. TO HIS UNCLE KING JOHN OF DENMARK (C. 1506)

*This singular letter was written on behalf of a tribe of gypsies who made their appearance at this date, and masquerading as pilgrims, imposed upon the credulity of James, who shows a truly mediæval ignorance of geographical conditions. It is probable that these were the first gypsies ever seen in the north. They migrated from the East into Europe about the beginning of the fifteenth century. We hear of them reaching Paris in 1427, also in the character of penitents. Later, they seem to have won considerable recognition in Scotland, for in 1535 we find James V. granting special protection to Johnie Faa, the hero of the well-known ballad, " and power to administer justice to his people conform to the law of Egypt."*

To the most illustrious, mighty, and serene Prince, John, by the mercy of God, King of Denmark, our uncle and brother and most beloved ally, James by the same grace of God, King of the Scots, wishes health and prosperity. Anthony Gawino, with other unfortunate and pitiable people who attend him in the course of his wanderings through the Christian world, impelled by the love of wandering, and, (as he states) in obedience to the command of the Apostolic See, some time ago drew near to the frontier of our Realm, beseeching us that he might be allowed without scaith to enter within our territory and have free course therein with all his gear and companions. It is easy to grant a boon when men are in harsh need. After having sojourned here some months right well, and, we are informed full Christianly, he is, O King and Uncle, making ready to journey into Denmark, but before crossing the sea he besought of us that we should inform your Highness thereof by letter, and at the same time commend the pitiable plight of his nation to your munificence.  Furthermore we believe that the history and race of wandering Egypt are better known unto you than unto us, by reason that Egypt is nearer to your kingdom ; also a greater number of men of this kind sojourn in your realm.

## FROM THE HOUSEHOLD BOOK OF JAMES IV.

*The connection subsisting between James IV. and the burgesses of Dumbarton was of the most intimate nature.  Hardly a year elapsed without his appearing among them either as a resident in the Castle or as a guest of some of the neighbouring nobles. His Household Book, which was carefully kept, shows that the King carried no money himself.*

1497, *April* 24.   Giffen to ane child that brocht apills to the King fra the provost of Dunbartane, IX. sh.

1504, *April*.   To John Forman, of the Wardrob, to pass fra Dunbartane to Strivelin, for the King's gear, 14 sh.

*April* 18.   In Dunbartane, to Martin, the Frenchman, for X. tun of wyne to the schippes vittaling in the Isles, ilk tun, IXX. lib.

*May* 18.   To the pyper of Dunbartane, XIV. sh.

1505, *May* 1.   To the King, to play at the cartis in Dunbartane with John Murray and Master Robert Cockburne, iiij. lib. X. sh.

That same nicht, to the evensang in the Kirk to the King himself in ane purse, XVI. sh.

1505, *July* 23.   Item, that day to ane man that brocht peirs to the King iiij. sh.

*Dec.* 8.   To bynding of Wallass's sword with cordis of

39

silk and new hilt and plomet, new skabbard, and new hilt to
the said sword, XXVj. sh.[1]

1506, *Aug.* 13. To the man that rowed the King over
the water iiij. sh.

*July* 24. To men that brocht strawberries and uther
berries to the King and Quene, Xiiij. sh.

### ELEGY ON THE DEATH OF BERNARD STEWART, LORD OF AUBIGNY (1508)

*Bernard Stewart came to Scotland in* 1484 *as French Ambassador, to renew the ancient league. A year later he led the
French auxiliaries who fought for Henry VII. at Bosworth.
Brantôme ranked him among the most illustrious of French
soldiers. He died in Edinburgh of a fever which he had con-
tracted in Calabria.*

> O duilfull death ! O dragon dolorous !
> Why hes thow done so dulfullie devoir
> The prince of knychtheid, nobill and chivilrous,
>   The witt of weiris, of armes and honour,
>   The crop of curage, the strength of armes in stour,
> The fame of France, the fame of Lumbardy,
>   The choiss of chiftanes, most awfull in armour,
> The carbunckell, cheif of every chevilrie !
>
> Pray now for him, all that him loveit heir !
> And for his saul mak intercession
> Unto the Lord that has him bocht so deir,
>   To gif him mercie and remissioun,

[1] The modern equivalent would be about £14. It was customary to
preserve the weapons of patriots and heroes, which were usually hung up
in churches. Shakespeare tells us in *Richard III.* :
  " Now are our brows bound with victorious wreaths
    Our bruiséd arms hung up for monuments."

And namelie we of Scottis natioun,
Intill his lyff whom most he did affy,
Forgett we nevir into our orisoun
To pray for him, the flour of chivelrie.

*William Dunbar.*


## ON THE CHANGES OF LYFE

Yisterday fair sprang the flowris,
This day thai ar all slane with schouris ;

.     .     .     .     .

So nixt to symmer wyntir bene,
Nixt efter confort cairis kene ;
Nixt efter midnycht myrthful morrow,
Nixt efter joy ay cumis sorrow.

*Idem.*


## HIS EPITAPH

I will nae priests for me shall sing,
Nor yet nae bells for me to ring,
But ae Bag-pype to play a spring.

*Walter Kennedy* (1460–1508).


## THE GREAT MICHAEL [1]

In this same year, (1511,) the King of Scotland built a ship
called the Great Michael, which was the greatest ship and

[1] The Great Michael was bought by Louis XII. on April 2nd, 1514,
for 40,000 livres, and never fired a gun for her own country.

of most strength that ever sailed in England or France ; for this ship was of so great stature, and took so much timber, that, except Falkland, she wasted all the woods in Fife, which were oakwood, over all the timber that was gotten out of Norway. For she was so strong, and of so great length and breadth (all the wrights of Scotland, yea, and many other strangers, were at her device by the King's commandment, who wrought very busily in her ; but it was year and day ere she was complete)—to wit, she was twelve score feet in length and thirty-six feet within the sides. She was ten feet thick in the wall, and had cut ribs of oak in her wall, and boards on every side, so strong and so thick, that no cannon could get through her. This great ship cumbered Scotland to get her to sea. When she was afloat, and her masts and sails complete, with ropes and anchors belonging thereto, she was counted to the King to be thirty thousand pounds of expenses by her artillery, which was very great and costly to the King, and by all the rest of her orders. She bare many cannons, six on each side ; with three great bassils, two behind in her dock, and one before ; with three hundred shot of small artillery, that is to say, myand, and battert-falcon, and quarter-falcon, slings, pestilent serpentens, and double dogs, with hagtor and culverin, cross-bows and hand-bows. She had three hundred mariners to sail her ; she had six score of gunners to use her artillery; and she had a thousand men of war, besides her captains, skippers, and quartermasters.

And if any man believe that this description of the ship be not of verity, as we have written, let him pass to the gate of Tullibardin, and there, before the same, he will see the length and breadth of her planted with hawthorn by the wright that helped to make her. As for the other properties of her, Sir

42

Andrew Wood [1] is my author, who was quartermaster of her, and Robert Barton,[2] who was master skipper.

This ship lay still in the roads ; and the King every day took pleasure to pass to her, and dine and sup in her with his lords, letting them see the order of his ship.

*Chronicles of Scotland, 1436–1565, by*
*Robert Lindsay of " Pitscottie."*

## LOVE LETTER FROM PERKIN WARBECK TO LADY KATHERINE GORDON (1496)

*Lady Katherine Gordon was singularly lovely.    We are told that Henry VII. " much marvelled at her beautiful and aimiable countenance " and called her the " White Rose."    She followed the fortunes of her husband, and with him was taken prisoner at St. Michael's Mount.*

Most noble lady, it is not without reason that all turn their eyes to you ; that all admire, love, and obey you.   For they see your two-fold virtues by which you are so much distinguished above all other mortals.   Whilst on the one hand they admire your riches and immutable prosperity, which secure to you the nobility of your lineage and the loftiness of your rank, they are on the other hand struck by your rather divine than human beauty, and believe that you are not born in our days, but descended from heaven.

All look at your face, so bright and serene that it gives splendour to the cloudy sky ; all look at your eyes as brilliant as stars, which make all pain to be forgotten, and turn despair into delight ; all look at your neck, which outshines pearls ;

[1] The famous naval commander, and Knight of Largo.
[2] The Bartons were the most skilled of Scottish seamen.   In 1506 Andrew sent three barrels full of pirates' heads to James IV. as an offering. But later, he became so wealthy that he was suspected of piracy himself.

all look at your fine forehead, your purple light of youth, your fair hair ; in one word, at the splendid perfection of your person ; and looking at, they cannot choose but admire you ; admiring, they cannot choose but love you ; loving, they cannot choose but obey you.

I shall, perhaps, be the happiest of all your admirers, and the happiest man on earth, since I have reason to hope you will think me worthy of your love. If I represent to my mind all your perfections, I am not only compelled to love, to adore, and to worship you, but love makes me your slave. Whether waking or sleeping, I cannot find rest or happiness except in your affection. All my hopes rest in you, and in you alone.

Most noble lady, my soul, look mercifully down upon me your slave, who has ever been devoted to you from the first hour he saw you. Love is not an earthly thing ; it is heaven born. Do not think it below yourself to obey love's dictates. Not only kings, but also gods and goddesses have bent their necks beneath its yoke.

I beseech you, most noble lady, to accept for ever one who in all things will cheerfully do your will as long as his days shall last. Farewell, my soul and my consolation. You, brightest ornament of Scotland, farewell, farewell.

*Translated from the Latin—B. M. Spanish*
*Calendars (Bergenroth).*


## LAMENT OF ERASMUS ON THE DEATH OF ALEXANDER STUART IN 1513

*Alexander Stuart (1494–1513), a natural son of James IV., was created Archbishop of St. Andrews and Primate of Scotland in his thirteenth year, and perished on the fatal field of*

*Flodden by the side of his father, before he was twenty. First taught by the elegant scholar David Paniter, and later by Erasmus at Padua, he excelled in all kinds of learning, and his physical beauty, too, was renowned. Tradition has it that on the night of his death he returned, spectrally, with a ghostly train of retainers, to sing his Requiem Mass before the High Altar of his own Cathedral.*

What hadst thou to do with Mars, of all the Gods of the poets the most infatuate, O thou, who wert the disciple of the Muses and of Christ?

## PROCLAMATION ISSUED ON SEPTEMBER 10TH, 1513

*This Municipal Proclamation was made at the City Cross as soon as the tragedy of Flodden reached Edinburgh, and all men, and as many women as were able, were impressed into the service of building a strong wall round the city, in order to bid defiance to the English, should they come. It shows the courageous and dignified spirit with which this national calamity was met.*

Forasmuch as there is a great rumour now lately risen within this town, touching our Sovereign Lord and his army, of which we understand there is come no verity as yet, wherefore we charge strictly and command, in our said Sovereign Lord, the King's name, and in that of the Presidents for the Provosts and Baillies within this burgh, that all manner of persons, townsmen within the same, have ready their arms of defence and weapons for war, and appear therewith before the said Presidents at the tolling of the common bell, for the keeping and defence of the town

45

against them that would invade the same. And we also charge that all women, and especially vagabonds, that they pass to their labours, and be not seen upon the street clamouring and crying, under the pain of banishing of their persons without favour, and that the other women of better sort pass to the kirk and pray, when time requires, for our Sovereign Lord and his army, and the townsmen who are with the army ; and that they hold them at their private labours off the streets within their houses, as becometh.

## JAMES V. HUNTS IN ATHOLL (1529)

The King, together with his mother and ane ambassadour of the Popes wha was in Scotland for the tyme, went all together to Atholl to the hunt. For this noble Earle of Atholl caused mak ane curious pallace to the King, his mother, and the ambassadour, whereby they were as weill eased [1] as if they had been in any pallace either of Scotland or Ingland, which was built in the middle of ane greene medow, and the walls thereof were of greene timber, woven with birks. The floores were laid with greene erthe and strewn with sic floures as grew in the medow, that no man knew whereon he ga'ed, bot as he had been in a greene garden. . . . This pallace was hung with fyne tapestrie within, and well lighted in all necessary parts with glass windows. The king was verrie well entertained in this wilderness the space of three days with all sic delicious and sumptuous meats as was to be had in Scotland.

*Robert Lindsay of " Pitscottie."*

[1] Comfortable.

46

## LETTER FROM SIR DAVID LINDSAY TO THE SECRETARY OF SCOTLAND (1531)

*Sir David Lindsay (1490–1555), known as the Juvenal of Scotland, was attached to the Court of James IV. and married Janet Douglas, the royal sempstress. For two centuries he was the poet of the Scottish people, and his works ranked next to the Bible in popularity. After he was appointed Lyon Herald (so called from the lion rampant in the Scottish regal escutcheon), he went as Envoy to several foreign countries, and in the following letter, written from the Netherlands where he had been sent to renew a commercial treaty of James I., describes the tournaments at the Court of Charles V.*

MY LORD,

I recommend my hearty service onto your Lordship. Please your Lordship to wit, that I came to Brussels the III. day of July, where I found the Emperor and got presence of His Majesty the third day after my coming, and have gotten good expedition of the principal errands that I was sent for ; and have gotten the old alliances, and confederations confirmed for the space of one hundred years. The which confirmation I have raised in double form, one to deliver to the Conservator, and one other to bring with me to Scotland, both under the Emperor's great seal. I remained at the Court seven weeks and odd days. Item, the bruit was here over all this country, when I came to the Court, that the King's Grace, our Sovreign, was dead. For the which cause the Queen of Hungary [1] sent for me, and enquired diligently of that matter from me, and was right glad when I showed her the verity of our King's Grace, our Sovreign's prosperity. It was showed to me that the Emperor's Majesty caused all

[1] Mary, Duchess of Hungary, sister of Charles V.

47

the churchmen in Brussels to pray for his Grace's soul. My Lord, it were too long to me to write to your Lordship the Triumphs I have seen, since coming to the Court Imperial ; that is to say the triumphant joustings, the terrible Tournaments, the fighting on foot in barras, (*a list of combatants*) the names of the lords and knights that were hurt the day of the great Tournament ; which circumstances I have written at length, in articles,[1] to shew the King's Grace at my homecoming. Item, the Emperor purposes to depart at the end of this month, and passes up in Almanye [2] for reformation of the Lutherans : the Queen of Hungary remains here Regent of all her countries : and was confirmed Regent by the three Estates in the town of Brussels, the fifth day of July. And as for the other news, I refer to bearer.

Written with my hand at Antwerp, at the XIII. day of August, by your Servitor, at his power,

DAVID LINDSAY, Herald to our Sovereign Lord.
(*Cotton Lib. Cal. B.I. fol.* 298.)

FROM "THE TESTAMENT OF SQUYER MELDRUN"

Fair weill, ye lemant [3] lampis of lustines
    Of fair Scotland, adew my Ladies all !
During my youth with ardent besines,
    Ye knaw how I was in your service thrall.
    Ten thowsand times adew above thame all
Sterne [4] of Stratherne, my Ladie Soverane !
For quhome I sched my blud with mekill pane.

---

[1] These articles have unfortunately not been preserved.
[2] Germany.        [3] Shining.        [4] Star.

48

Yit wald my Ladie luke at even and morrow
  On my legend, at length scho wald not mis
How for hir saik I sufferit mekill sorrow.
Yit if I micht at this time get my wis,
  Of hir sweit mouth, deir God, I had ane kis.
I wish in vane, allace we will dissever,
I say na mair, Sweit hart, adew for ever !

*Idem.*


### ADVICE TO HIS PUPIL JAMES V.

Wherefore, *sen* [1] thou has *sic* capacity
  To learn to play so pleasantly, and sing,
Ride horse, run spears, with great audacity,
  Shoot with hand-bow, cross-bow, and culvering,
AMONG THE REST, SIR, LEARN TO BE A KING !

*From " The Monarchia."*


### FROM ''THE GREAT CURSING'' (c. 1532)

*In the Church of Rome sentence of excommunication was
usually delivered in Latin, but Gavin Dunbar, Archbishop of
Glasgow, issued this " monition of cursing " in the vernacular,
and all the priests of the Border parishes were instructed to read
it from the altar and from the market Cross. It was used
against any who had offended against Church law.*

I curse their head and all the hairs of their head, I curse
their face, their eyes, their mouth, their nose, their tongue,
their teeth, their shoulders, their back, and their heart,
their arms, their legs, their hands, their feet, and every part
of their body, from the top of their head to the sole of their

[1] Since.

N.S.                               49                              E feet. Before and behind, within and without. I curse them walking and I curse them riding. I curse them standing and I curse them sitting. I curse them eating and I curse them drinking, I curse them waking and I curse them sleeping. I curse them within the house and I curse them without the house. I curse their wives, their bairns and their servants. I curse their cattle, their wool, their sheep, their horse, their swine, their geese, and their hens. I curse their halls, their chambers, their stables and their barns. The malediction of God that lit upon Lucifer, that struck him from the high Heaven to the deep Hell shall light upon them. The fire and the sword that stopped Adam from the gates of Paradise shall stop them from the gloir of Heaven until they forbear and make amends. I dissever, and part them from the Kirk of God, and deliver them quick [1] to the devill of Hell, as the Apostle Paul delivered Corinthion.[2] And finally, I condemn them perpetually to the deep pit of Hell, to remain with Lucifer and all his fellows. And as these candles go from your sight, so may their souls go from the visage of God, and their good frame from the world, until they forbear their open sins and rise from this terrible cursing and make satisfaction and penance.

*Brit. Mus. State Papers, Henry VIII., Vol. IV.*

[1] Living.
[2] See in St. Paul's I. Cor. 5, the episode of a certain incestuous Corinthian (Κορίνθιον) whom St. Paul consigned to Satan.

# PART II

Πῶς τις ἄνευ θανάτου σε φύγοι, βίε.

*Æsop, VI. Cent. B. C.*

Life is a passing shadow; the shadow of a bird in its flight.

*The Talmud.*

Nothing is more certen to man than death, but nothing is more uncerten than the houre of death.

*Richard Beauforest (fl.* 1554).

One doth but breakfast here, another dine, he that lives longest does but suppe; we must all go to bed in another world.

*Bishop Henshawe (fl.* 1631).

Lest pride besiege our hearts let us think on the epitaph of Alcuin, the dear friend and teacher of Charlemagne.
" *Quod nunc es, fueram, famosus in orbe, viator,*
*Et quod nunc ego sum, tuque futurus eris. . . .*"

*Anon.*

There are no fields of amaranth on this side of the grave; there are no voices, O Rhodope, that are not soon mute, however tuneful; there is no name with whatever emphasis of passionate love repeated, of which the echo is not faint at last. . . .

*Walter Savage Landor.*

51                                              E 2

# TWO SONGS

*These beautiful songs, thought to date from the earlier part of
the sixteenth century, are included in the " Cantus, Songs, and
Fancies, to severall Musicall Parts " . . . which, printed by
John Forbes in Aberdeen (1682), was the first collection of
secular music published in Scotland.*

## I

In a garden so green in a May-morning,
Heard I my lady pleen [1] of paramours,
Said she : " My love so sweet, come you not yet, not yet ?
Heght [2] you not to me to meet amongst the flowers ? "
*Eloré, Eloré, Eloré, Eloré,*
*I love my lusty love, Eloré, lo !*

" The light up springeth, the dew down dingeth,
The sweet larks singeth their hours of prime,
Phebus up sprenteth, [3] joy to rest wenteth,
So lost is mine intents, and gone's the time."
*Eloré, etc. . . .*

" Danger my dead is, false fortune my feed is,
And languor my leid [4] is, but hope I dispair,
Disdain my desire is, so strangeness my fear is,
Deceit out of all ware !—Adew, I fare ! "
*Eloré, etc. . . .*

[1] Complain.          [2] Promised.
[3] Springeth.          [4] Bondage.

53

Then to my lady blyth did I my presence kyth,[1]
Saying : " My bird, be glad : am I not yours ? "
So in my armes two [2] did I the lusty jo,[3]
And kissed her mo than night hath hours.
*Eloré, etc.* . . .

" Live in hope, ladie fair, and repel all dispair,
Trust not that your true love shall you betray,
When deceit and languor banisht is from your bowr,
I'le be your paramour and shal you please."
*Eloré, etc.* . . .

" Favour and dutie unto your bright beautie
Confirmed hath lawtie [4] obliedged to truth,
So that your soverance, heartelie but variance,
Mark in your memorance mercie and ruth."
*Eloré, etc.* . . .

" Yet for your courtesie, banish all jealousie,
Love for love lustily do me restore,
Then with us lovers young true love shal rest and reign,
Solace shall sweetly sing for evermore ! "
*Eloré, etc.* . . .

## II

The Gowans [5] are gay, my jo ;
*The Gowans are gay,*
They make me wake when I should sleep,
*The first morning of May.*

[1] Make known.　　　　　　　[2] Two arms.
[3] Love.　　　　　　　　　　　[4] Loyalty.
[5] Daisies.

54

About the fields as I did pass,
*The gowans are gay ;*
I chanced to meet a proper Lass,
*The first morning of May.*

Right busie was that bonny maid,
*The gowans are gay ;*
And I thereafter to her said,
*The first morning of May.*

O Ladie fair, what do you here ?
*The gowans are gay ;*
Gathering the dew, what needs you spear ?
*The first morning of May.*

The dew, quoth I, what can that mean ?
*The gowans are gay ;*
She said, To wash my Ladie clean,
*The first morning of May.*

I asked farther at her sine,
*The gowans are gay ;*
To my will if you would incline,
*The first morning of May.*

She said her errand was not there,
*The gowans are gay ;*
Her maidenhead on me to ware,
*The first morning of May.*

Thus left I her and past my way,
*The gowans are gay ;*
Into a garden me to play,
*The first morning of May.*

55

Where there were birds singing full sweet,
*The gowans are gay ;*
Unto me comfort was full meet,
*The first morning of May.*

And thereabout I past my time,
*The gowans are gay ;*
While that it was the hour of Prime,
*The first morning of May.*

And then returned home agan,
*The gowans are gay ;*
Pensing what maiden that had been,
*The first morning of May.*

## OLD INSCRIPTION

*The following lines are on the ancient pre-Reformation bell preserved in St. Giles' Cathedral, Edinburgh. According to tradition, bells, in those days, were rung, not merely to call the people to their prayers, but also as a deliberate offensive against the Devil, who, being Prince of the Powers of the Air, was scared by the voices of consecrated bells vibrating through his dominion. For this reason they were rung on the approach of " great tempestes or lightninges."*

O MATER DEI

MEMENTO MEI.

Anno : D : M : IIII.

LETTER FROM LORD MAXWELL (LORD WARDEN
OF THE WEST MARCHES OF SCOTLAND) TO
LORD DACRE (LORD WARDEN OF THE WEST
MARCHES OF ENGLAND) (1550)

*In this letter Lord Maxwell, who is about to accompany
Marie de Guise to France on a visit to her daughter Mary,
then eight years old, " desires a meeting for the reformation
of injuries, and the establishment of quietness on the Marches."
The regulation of the Borders by distinct laws, under the rule
of lords wardens of the marches, commenced in the reign of
Edward I., at the time when he affected the sovereignty over
Scotland. Hostilities were ceaseless, and the tenants of the
different manors were obliged, upon the firing of beacons, to
attend their Lord in the service of the Borders at their own
expense ; which service might be prolonged for forty days.[1]
One of their ancient oaths began very finely : " I swear by the
Heaven above me, Hell beneath me, by my part of Paradise, and
by all that God made in six days and seven nights, and by God
himself. . . ."*

After my lawful commendations, it would please your
lordship to be advertised, that among other gentlemen of this

---

[1] Here is a Proclamation made at Penrith, June 14th, 1547, for raising
the power of the Borders.

" Forasmuch as the Governor of Scotland, Arran, their Queen (Marie
de Guise, widow of James V.) and other noblemen of that realm, repaired
to Pebles upon Sunday at night last, and also their ordnance coming from
Edinburgh, of intent with a great army of the whole body of the said
realm of Scotland to do some enterprize against the King's Majesty's
possessions and subjects upon these West Marches : Therefore Lord
Wharton Lord Warden of the West Marches of England for anempst
Scotland, strictly chargeth and commandeth, in his Majesty's name, that
all his subjects, horsemen, and footmen within the bounds of the said
West Marches, prepare their arediness, and come forward with ten days
victuals, so as they may be at Carlisle upon Thursday next at noon, not
failing hereof upon pain of death. God save the King."

country, I am commanded for one, to go with the Queen into France, and seeing our passage is so shortly, that I may not have time to meet your lordship at a day of Marche, for the reforming of such attempts as are done on both the Borders, I am desirous, if it be your pleasure, to wait upon you on Friday next, to come to Tordawath at eight o'clock before noon, in quiet manner, with fifty horse, to the intent that we may commune together for the better stay of both the princes subjects. My lord, it is not unknown to you, as I trust, that there is a conduct granted for 200 horses of the Queen's company to go through England ; and as ye know it is a far way to me to send my horse about by Berwick, wherefore I will desire, if it be your pleasure, that ye will suffer four horse of mine and two servants to go in at Carlisle hand, and meet with the rest of the Queen's horse at Borrow-briggs. And what your pleasure is, I pray you give me advertisement with speed, for I must shortly depart. And thus I commit you to God.

From Dumfries, this Wednesday at night the 27th of August.

> Your lordship's lefully,
> R. MAXWELL.

## PRAYER TO BE SAID AT THE LORD'S SUPPER

O Lord, we acknowledge that no creature is able to comprehend the length and breadth, the deepness and height, of Thy most excellent love, which moved Thee to show mercy where none was deserved ; to promise and give life where Death had gotten victory ; to receive us into Thy grace when we could do nothing but rebel against Thy justice. O Lord, the blind dullness of our corrupt nature will not suffer us

58

sufficiently to weigh these Thy most ample benefits ; yet nevertheless, at the commandment of Jesus Christ our Lord, we present ourselves to this his Table to declare and witness before the world that by him alone we have received liberty and life ; that by him alone we have entrance to the throne of thy grace ; that by him alone we are possessed in our spiritual kingdom, to eat and drink at his Table ; with whom we have our conversation presently in Heaven ; and by whom our bodies shall be raised up again from the dust, and shall be placed with him in that endless joy, which Thou, O Father of mercy, hast prepared for thine elect, before the foundation of the world was laid. And these most inestimable benefits we acknowledge and confess to have received of Thy free mercy and grace, by Thy only beloved Son Jesus Christ, for the which therefore, we thy Congregation, moved by Thy Holy Spirit, render Thee all thanks, praise, and glory, for ever and ever.

*John Knox* (1505–1572).

## LETTER FROM JOHN KNOX TO HIS MOTHER, MRS. ELIZABETH BOWES, NOVEMBER 4TH, 1555.

*In 1555 John Knox returned for a short time to Scotland, after his imprisonment in France, for being concerned in the slaughter of Cardinal Beaton at St. Andrews in 1546. He made a successful preaching tour which lasted ten months.*

The wayes of man are not in his own power.

Albeit my journey toward Scotland, beloved Mother, was most contrarious to my own judgement, before I did enterprise the same, yet this day I praise God for her who was the

59

cause external of my resort to these quarters ; that is, I praise God in you, and for you, whom he made the instrument to draw me from the den of my own ease (you alone did draw me from the rest of quiet study) to contemplate and behold the fervent thirst of our brethren, night and day sobbing and groaning for the bread of life. If I had not seen it with my eyes in my own country, I could not have believed it—I praised God when I was with you, perceiving that in the midst of Sodom, God hath more Lots than one, and more faithful daughters than two. But the fervency here doth far exceed all others that I have seen ; and therefore shall patiently bear, although I spend here yet some days ; for depart I cannot until such time as God quench their thirst a little. Yea, Mother, their fervency doth so ravish me, that I cannot but accuse and condemn by slothful coldness. God grant them their heart's desire ! And I pray you advertise of your estate, and of things that have occurred since your last writing. Comfort yourself in God's promises, and be assured, that God stirs up more friends than we be aware of. I commit you to the protection of the Omnipotent.

In great haste, the 4th of November 1555, from Scotland.

Your son,

JOHN KNOX.

## A BIDDING PRAYER[1] IN WHICH PEACE WITH SCOTLAND IS PRAYED FOR (1546)

First ye shall pray for the whole congregation of the true Christian and Catholic Church of Christ. And specially for this Church of England and Ireland. Wherein, first I commend to your devout prayers our most Sovreign Lorde the

[1] Used in England in the reign of Edward VI.

King, supreme head in earthe, immediately under God, that God, for his great mercy send him grace to govern and to rule this realm. And for Queen Katerine dowagier. And also for my lady Mary, and my lady Elizabethe the King's sisters. Ye shall also make your hartie and effectual prayer to Almighty God, for the peace of all Christian regions, *and especially, that the most joyfull and perpetual peace and unity of this realm and Scotland may shortly be perfected and brought to pass, by the most Godly and happy marriage of the King's Majesty and the young Queen of Scotland.*[1] *And that it would please the Almighty to aid with strength, wisdom, and power, and with his holy defence, all those who favoreth and setteth forward the same, and weaken and confound all those which laboreth or studyeth to the interruption of so godly a quiet, whereof both these two realmes should take so great a benefit and profit.* Secondly ye shall pray for my Lord Protector's grace ; and for Lord Archbishop of Canterbury for all the lords spiritual and temporal of this realm, for master Mayor of this city, with all his brethren and the commons of the same. Also ye shall pray for the peace both on land and water, that God grant love and charity among all Christian people. Thirdly, ye shall pray God for all them that be departed out of this world, in the faith of Christ, that they with us, and we with them, at the Day of Judgement, may rest both body and soul, with Abraham, Isaac, and Jacob, in the Kingdom of Heaven.

*Amen.*

[1] In 1543, the Protector Somerset undertook an expedition into Scotland in the hopes of compelling the government of that country to fulfil the treaty entered into with Henry VIII. for the marriage of the young Queen, Mary Stuart (who was only one year old), to his only son Prince Edward " being then not past six years of age." The negociations failed, and she was conveyed to France " to be knit in marriage with Francis, then Dolphin, but before he expired, King of France."

## PROPOSAL FOR THE RETURN OF MARY STUART TO SCOTLAND

*Mary was born at Linlithgow on December 8th, 1542, while her father, James V., was dying, brokenhearted after his defeat at Solway Moss. When he was told that he had a " fair daughter " he answered : " Adieu, farewell. . . . It came with a lass, and it will pass with a lass. . . . And so he recommended himself to the mercy of Almighty God, and spake little from that time forth, but turned his back unto his lords, and his face unto the wall, and in this manner departed." He referred to Marjory, daughter of Robert Bruce, who on her marriage with Walter, sixth Steward, in 1315, brought the crown of Scotland to his family ; but this prophecy was unfulfilled, the change of title taking place under James, and not at Mary's death.*

*The little Queen went to France at the age of six and was brought up in the midst of exotic gaieties at the cynical Court of Henri II., where her taste for letters was carefully fostered. Anne d'Este, Princess of Ferrara, tells us that at seven years old " her talk and carriage were so discreet that we no longer treated her as a child," and at thirteen she made a speech in Latin in the hall of the Louvre, the MS. of which has unfortunately perished. Ronsard [1] was her intimate friend and favourite poet, and he best describes her beauty in these incomparable lines :*

*" Ses yeux étoilés, deux beaux logis d'amour,*
*Qui feroyent d'une nuit le midi d'un beau jour." . . .*

*In 1558, she married the Dauphin, afterwards Francis II.,*

[1] This friendship continued all through her life, and she became one of his two Royal Egerias. Even when the wheel of fortune turned, she managed to send him, from the depths of her northern prison, in 1583, " un buffet de deux mille écus," which bore an inscription : " A Ronsard, l'Apollon de la Source des Muses."

*who two years later " departed to God, leaving as heavy and dolorous a wife, as of right she had good cause to be, who by long watching with him during his sickness, and painful diligence about him, and specially by the issue thereof, is not in best tune of her body, but without danger." Mary was then aged eighteen.*

Now that death hath thus disposed of the late French King, whereby the Scottish Queen is left a widow, one of the special things your Lordships have to consider, and to have an eye to, is the marriage of that Queen. During her husband's life there was no great account made of her, for that being under bond of marriage and subjection of her husband (who carried the burden and care of all matters) there was offered no great occasion to know what was in her. But since her husband's death she hath showed (and so continueth) that she is both of great wisdom for her years, modesty, and also of great judgment in the wise handling herself and her matters, which, increasing with her years, cannot but turn greatly to her commendation, reputation, honour, and great benefit of her and her country. . . . Immediately upon her husband's death she changed her lodging, withdrew herself from all company, and became so solitary and exempt of all worldliness that she doth not to this day see daylight, and so will continue out forty days.

*From Sir Nicholas Throckmorton (Ambassador to Scotland), to the Council—Foreign Calendar—Elizabeth.*

## MARY'S OPINION OF SCOTLAND BEFORE SHE LANDED IN 1561

The countrie of Scotland shee esteemed not soe farr inferiour to France as a private persone is inferiour to a prince. And that for twoe respects that countrie did suite well anough with her likeing, one, for that it was the place of her birth, the other for that it was the seate of her sovereigntie. The disorderes which had sometyme beene raysed by the people, shee much imputed to unskilfull gouernment, in striving to reduce them to a stricter subjectione then that whereto they had beene accustomed. But, whensoever ther kings attempted not to impeach ther liberty, they lived without danger of honor, or of life ; they wer not onely mainteined free from inward tumultes, but made invincible against ther enemyes. Shee nothing mistrusted the disability of her sexe ; for, besides a generall respect that men beare towardes women, in regard whereof many people would bee governed onely by princes of that sexe ; besides her large indowments of nature, a lovely and lively countenance, a fayre feature, fine and percing witt, a mild and modest dispositione, and then in the flower of beauty and youth (*strong strings to draw men to duty and love*) ; besides an affable and curteous behaviour, fashioned by her educatione in the court of France,—shee intended not to make any alteratione from the present state of affayres in Scotland. Soe shee prepared for her passage, and in the meane tyme went into Lorraine to take leave of her kindred by the motheres side.

*From " Annals of the First Four Years of the Reign of Elizabeth," by Sir John Hayward, Knt., D.C.L., 1599.*

MARY ASKS FOR A PASSPORT (1561)

*Mary sent to Elizabeth for a safe conduct, in case she should be forced by any accident to land in England. This was granted, and " the Queen of Scotts, having the advantage both of a great calm and thicke mist, adventured to sea in certayne French gallies, and arrived safely in the road of Leith."*

The Queen of Scotland, Queen Dowager of France, desires to obtain the following from her good sister, the Queen of England, and has charged M. D'Oysel to the same effect :—

1. A passport for her, with a clause that if she arrives in any part of England, she may tarry there, and purchase provisions and necessaries, and if it seems good to her, that she may leave her ships and pass by land to Scotland.

2. Another safe conduct for her to pass through England to Scotland with her train, and one hundred horses, mules, &c.

*Foreign Calendar—Elizabeth.*

## A BALLAD OF WELCOME

*On September 2nd, 1561, when Mary made her entry into Edinburgh, she was presented with a Bible and a Psalter " coverit with fine purpour velvet," and the keys of the gates. The following verses were spoken to " la belle et doulce reyne " by a boy of six years of age :*

Welcome, O Souveraine ! Welcome, O natyve Quene !
Welcome to us your subjects great and small !
Welcome, I say, even from the verie splene,[1]
    To Edinburgh your syttie principall.

[1] Heart.

Whereas your people with harts both one and all
Doth herein offer to your excellence
 Two proper volumes in memoriall
As gyfte most gainand to a godlie prince.


Wherein your Grace may reade to understande
 The perfett waye unto the hevennes hie,
And how to rule your subjects and your land,
 And how your kingdom stablished shal be,
 Judgment and wysdome therein shall ye see,
Here shall you find your God his due commande,
 And who the contrarie does wilfullie,
How them he threatens with his scurge and wand.


Ane gyfte more precious could we none present
 Nor yet more needefull to your Excellence,
Qwylk is Gode's lawes his words and testament
 Trewlie translate with frutefull diligence,
 Qwylk to accepte with humble reverence
The Provist present most hartelie you exorte
 With the hole subjects due obedience,
Together with the keys of their porte.


In signe that they and all that they possess
 Bodie and good shall ever reddie be
To serve you as their souveraine hie mistress
 Both daye and night after thair bound dutie :
 Beschinge your Grace in this necessitie
Their too shorte tyme and their godwill consether
 Accepte their harts and take it pacientlie
That may be done, seeing all is yours together.

## A NEW YEAR GIFT TO QUEEN MARY (1562)

*The following stanzas, taken from a long poem addressed to Mary, illustrate the loyal feelings with which she was regarded.*

Welcome, illustrate Ladye, and our Queen ;
Welcome our Lion with the Fleur-de-Lis ;
Welcome our Thistle with the Lorraine green ;
Welcome our rubent Rose upon the rise ;
Welcome our Gem, and joyful Genetrice ;
Welcome our Belle of Albion to bear ;
Welcome our pleasant Princess maist of price !
God give you grace against this good New Year.

This good New Year we hope, with grace of God,
Shall be of peace, tranquillity, and rest ;
This year shall Right and Reason rule the Rod,
Which so long season has been sore supprest ;
This year firm Faith shall freely be confess'd,
And all erroneous questions put arrear ;
To labour that this Life among us left,
God give you grace against this good New Year.

Now to conclude, on Christ cast thy comfort,
And cherish them that thou hast under charge,
Suppose most sure He shall send thee support,
And lend thee lusty Liberos at large ;
Believe the Lord can harbour so thy barge,
To make broad Britain blyth as bird on brier,
And thee extol with his triumphant targe,[1]
Victoriously agane this good New Year.

Alexander Scott (1525–1584).

[1] Shield.

FRAGMENT

Return hamewart my heart again
And byde quhair thou was wont to be.
Thou art a fool to suffer pain,
For luve of her that luves not thee.

*Idem.*

## THE DEATH OF CHÂTELAR (1563)

*Pierre de Boscosel de Châtelar, a hapless musician and poet, grandnephew of the Chevalier Bayard, came to Scotland with Mary as her page and addressed poems to his royal mistress, who replied to them graciously and encouraged his affection, " often making him good cheer, and entertaining hum." The tale of his tragic end at the age of 23 is told by Brantôme in his " Dames Galantes : " " Et le jour venu, ayant esté mené sur l'eschafaut, advant mouryr, avoyt en ses mains les Hymnes de Monsr de Ronsard et, pour son eternelle consolation, se mist à lire tout entierement l'Hymne de la mort, qui est très bien fait et propre pour fayre aborrer la mort, ne s'aydant autrement d'autre livre spirituel, ny de ministre ny de confesseur. Aprez avoyr fait son entyere lecture, se tournait vers le lieu où il pensoit que la reyne fust, il s'escria haut : ' Adieu la plus belle et la plus cruelle princesse de ce monde !' et puys, fort constamment, tendant le cou à l'executeur, se layssa defayre fort aysement."*

*It was very rare in those days to refuse the offices of religion, and to choose a poem as a preparation for death.*

Amongst the minions of the court there was one named Monsieur Chatelar, a Frenchman, that at that time passed all others in credit with the Queen. In dancing of the *Purpose* (so term they that dance, in the which man and woman talk secretly . . .) in this dance, the Queen chose Chatelar, and Chatelar took the Queen. Chatelar had the best dress. All this winter, Chatelar was so familiar in the Queen's cabinet, early and late, that scarcely could any of the nobility have access unto her. The Queen would lie upon Chatelar's shoulder, and sometimes privily she would steal a kiss of his neck. And all this was honest enough ; for it was the gentle entreatment of a stranger. But the familiarity was so great, that upon a night, he privily did convoy himself under the Queen's bed ; but being espied, he was commanded away. The bruit [report] arising, the Queen called the Earl of Murray, and bursting into a womanly affection, charged him, that, as he loved her, he should slay Chatelar, and let him never speak a word. The other at first made promise so to do . . . but returned and fell upon his knees before the Queen and said : Madam, I beseech your Grace cause not me to take the blood of this man upon me ; your Grace has entreated him so familiarly before, that you have offended all your nobility ; and now, if he shall be secretly slain at your own commandment, what shall the world judge of it ? I shall bring him to the presence of justice, and let him suffer by law according to his deserving. " Oh," said the Queen, " you will never let him speak." I shall do (said he), madam, what in me lieth to save your honour.

Poor Chatelar was brought back from Kinghorn to St. Andrews, examined, put to an assize, and so beheaded, the 22nd day of February, 1563. He begged license to write to France the cause of his death, which, said he, in his tongue was, *Pour estre trouvé en lieu trop suspect ;* that is, Because I was found in a place too much suspected. At the place of execution, when he saw that there was no remedy but death, he made a godly confession, and granted that his declining from the truth of God, and following of vanity and impiety, was justly recompensed upon him. But in the end he concluded, looking unto the heavens, with these words, *O cruel dame!* that is, cruel mistress! What that complaint imported, lovers may divine. And so received Chatelar the reward of his dancing, for he lost his head, that his tongue should not utter the secrets of our Queen. *Deliver us, O Lord, from the rage of such inordinate rulers.*

*From John Knox's " History of the Reformation."*

### A LAMENT FOR DARNLEY

*Lord Darnley met with his death on February* 10*th,* 1567. *" A little after midnight, the house wherein the King lodged was in an instant blown in the air, he lying sleeping in his bed, with such a vehemency, that of the whole lodging, walls, and other, there is nothing remained, no, not a stone above another, but all carried far away or dashed in dross to the very groundstone."* *It was afterwards made public that this had been done by the command of the Earls of Bothwell and Morton. The following ballad, which shows that Mary was suspected of instigating the crime, was used as a political weapon against her.*

To Edinburgh about six hours at morn,
   As I was passing pansand [1] out the way ;
Ane bonny boy was sore making his moan,
   His sorry song was " Oche, and Wallaway !
That ever I should lyve to see that day,
Ane king at eve, with sceptre, sword and crown ;
   At morn but a deformed lump of clay,
With traitors strong so cruelly put down ! "

[1] Thinking.

Then drew I near some tidings for to speir,
    And said, " My friend, what makis thee sa way [1] ? "
" Bloody Bothwell hath brought our king to beir,
    And flatter and fraud with double Dallilay.
At ten houris on Sunday late at een,
    When Dalila and Bothwell bade good night,
Off her finger false she threw ane ring,
    And said, My Lord, ane token you I plight.

" I ken right well ye knaw your duty,
    Gif ye do not purge you ane and all,
Then shall I write in pretty poetry,
    In Latin laid in style rhetorical ;
    Which through all Europe shall ring like ane bell,
In the contempt of your malignity.
    Fye, flee fra Clytemnestra fell,
For she was never like Penelope.

" With Clytemnestra I do not fain to fletch,
    Who slew her spouse, the great Agamemnon ;
Or with any that Ninu's wife doth match,
    Semiramis quha brought her gude lord down.
    Quha do abstain fra litigation,
Or from his paper hald aback the pen ?
    Except he hate our Scottish nation,
Or then stand up and traitors deeds commend ?

" Now all the woes that Ovid in Ibin,[2]
    Into his pretty little book did write,
And many more be to our Scottish Queen,
    For she the cause is of my doleful dyte.

[1] Sad.
[2] Ibis.  Ovid wrote a poem of this name in which there is a terrific
number of curses.

71

Sa may her heart be fillet full of syte,
As Hero was for Leander's death ;
Herself to slay for woe who thought delyte,
For Henry's sake to like our Queen was laith.

" The dolours alas that pierced Dido's heart,
When King Enee from Carthage took the flight,
For the which cause unto a brand she start,
And slew herself, which was a sorry sight,
Sa might she die as did Creusa bright,
The worthy wife of douty Duke Jason ;
Wha brint was in ane garment wrought by slight [1]
Of Medea through incantation.

" Her laughter light be like to true Thisbe
When Pyramus she found dead at the well,
In languor like unto Penelope,
For Ulysses who long at Troy did dwell.
Her dolesome death be worse than Jezebel,
Whom through an window surely men did thraw ;
Whose blood did lap the cruel hundis fell,
And doggis could her wicked bainis [2] gnaw.

" Were I an hound—oh ! if she an hare,
And I an cat, and she a little mouse,
And she a bairn, and I a wild wod bear,
I an ferrit, and she cuniculus. [3]
To her I shall be aye contrarius—
When to me Atropus cut the fatal thread,
And fell deithis dartys dolorous,
Then shall our spirits be at mortal feid.

[1] Cleverness.          [2] Bones.          [3] Rabbit.

" My spirit her spirit shall duck in Phlegethon,[1]
Into that painful filthy flood of hell,
And then in Styx, and Lethe baith anone—
And Cerberus that cruel hound sa fell,
Sall gar her cry with mony gout and yell,
O Wallaway ! that ever she was born,
Or with treason by ony manner mell,[2]
Whilk from all bliss should cause her be forlorn."

*From Maidment's " Scottish Songs and Ballads."*

## LETTER FROM MARY TO SIR ROBERT MELVILLE. LOCHLEVEN, 1567

*The royal captive being destitute of wearing apparel wrote to her former Lord Chamberlain begging him to send her some necessaries ; but it was not till the following year that her request for the three gowns was granted.*

ROBERT MELWYNE.—Ye shall not fail to send with this bearer to me half-ell of *incarnatt* satin and half-ell of *blew* satin ; also cause Servais[3] my *Concierge* send me more twined silk gif there rests any, and sewing gold, and sewing silver; also ane doublet and skirts of white satin, ane other incarnat, ane other of black satin, and the skirts with them. Send na skirt with the red doublet. Also ane loose gown of taffateis ; also ye shall send the gown and the other clothes that I bade the Lady Lethington *gar* send me. Also ye shall not fail to send my maidens' clothes, for they are naked, and marvel ye have not sent them since your departing fra me, together with the

---

[1] The burning river of Hell.    [2] Meddle.
[3] Servais de Condé was the keeper of the Queen's wardrobe

*camaraige*[1] and linen cloth whereof I gave you ane memorial; and gif the *schone*[2] be not ready made, cause send them with some other after. Also ye shall cause Servais send twa pair sheets, with twa ounce black sewing silk ; also cause him to send me all the dry damask plums that he has, together with the pears he has ; this ye shall not fail to do. Ye shall cause make ane dozen of raising needles and moulds, and send me. And speir at Servais gif he has any other covering of beds *to* me *nor grein*,[3] and send me to put under the tother covering. I marvel ye forget to send me silver, conform to promise.

*Melville Papers.*

LETTER FROM MARY TO CHARLES IX.
*From her prison at Carlisle,* 1568.

MONSIEUR MON BON FRÈRE,

Le sieur de Monmorin ne m'a aporté peu de consolation en l'extresmité de ma misère de me venir visiter et s'enquerir de mon estast, qui despand de Dieu et de votre ayde, comme il vous pourra declarer au long. Car, je ne vous veulx importuner de longues lamantations. Mays je vous diray seullement que j'ay estay trété le plus indignemant que fut jamays non princesse mays gentill fame et avecq le plus d'injustice, ayant esté calomniée le plus faulsement ; et non seullemant cela mays en dangier de ma vie, si Dieu ayant pitié de mon inossance et conoissance de leur faulseté ne m'eut sauvée de leur mayns.

Par quoy je vous suplie avoir esguard à ma necesité et me voulloir ayder comme je prie se porteur vous fayre entendre le besoign que j'en ay. Et j'espère vous fayre paroistre leur inventions faulses et tendant à la ruine de moy et tous princes

[1] Cambric.     [2] Shoes.     [3] Green.

74

prinsipallemant tenant l'ansiene religion en laquelle j'espère mourir.

Et pour ce que j'e si grand besoign de votre secours promptemant, j'en feray d'autant plus brieff discours me remetant à votre embassadeur et a la sufisance de ce porteur me recommandant bien . . .

*Paris, Bibliothèque Nationale.*

## FROM THE FAREWELL SERMON OF JOHN KNOX (1571)

What I have been to my country, albeit this unthankful age will not know, yet the ages to come will be compelled to bear witness to the truth.

## AT THE BURIAL OF JOHN KNOX (1572)

Here lies one who neither feared nor flattered any flesh.

*James Douglas, Earl of Morton.*

## LETTER FROM GEORGE BUCHANAN TO RANDOLPH SQUIAR, MINISTER OF POSTES TO THE QUEEN'S GRACE OF ENGLAND (1577)

*The fame of George Buchanan (1506–1582) as a " polite writer and a man of deep learning and solid judgment " is established on lasting foundations, and he was honoured in foreign countries as a Latin scholar. He lived at a time, of course, when lectures and sermons could be delivered in that language. While studying for his degree at the great University of Paris in 1526, his fellow students were Rabelais, Loyola, Calvin and Francisco Xavier, " the Apostle of the Indies," The amount of Latin writing from the fifteenth to the seventeenth century was immense in bulk, outweighing the entire extant classical literature. Mary appointed Buchanan tutor to James VI., who cordially disliked him, and styled his history " an infamous invective."*

MAISTER.—I haif received diverse letters from you, and yet I have ansourit to none of thayme ; of the quhylke albeit I have many excusis as age, forgetfulness, business and disease, yet I wyl use none now except my sweirness (*laziness*) and your gentilness ; and if ye thynk none of these sufficient, content you with a confession of the fault, without fear of punitioun to follow on my unkindness. As for the present, I am occupied in writyng of our Historie, being assured to content few and to displease mony there through. As to the end of it, yf ye gett it not ere thys winter be passit, lippen (*depend*) not for it or none other writings from me. The rest of my occupation is wyth the gout, which holds me busy both day and nycht. And quhair ye say ye have not long to live, I traist to God to go before you, albeit I be on foot, and ye ryd the post. And thus I take my leif shortly from you now ; and my lang leif quhen God pleases, committing you to the protection of the Almychty. At Sterling, XXV. day of August, 1577.

Yours to command with service,

G. BUCHANAN.

## EPIGRAM

*This verse, by George Buchanan, alludes, it is presumed, to the diamond ring, originally given by Queen Elizabeth to Mary, as a pledge of affection and support, which Mary returned to her, when she determined to seek an asylum in England. John Aubrey, the antiquarian, tells us that " the heart was two diamonds, which joyned made the heart ; Queen Elizabeth kept*

*one moietie, and sent the other as a token of her constant friend-*
*ship to Mary Queen of Scotts : but she cutt off her head for*
*all that.*"

> Quod te jampridem fruitur, videt, ac amat absens,
> Hæc pignus cordis gemma, et imago mei est ;
> Non est candidior, non est hæc purior illo,
> Quamvis dura magis, non mage firma tamen.

### SUPERSTITION[1] AGAINST MARRYING IN MAY

That poor silly Jeezabel, our Queen Mary, married that
lang-legged ne'er-do-weel, Darnley, in the month of May,
and ever sin syne the Scots folks have regarded it as no
canny.

*Reginald Dalton.*

### AN OPINION

A dead woman bites not.

*Master of Gray, Scottish Envoy* (1585), *in a statement*
*soliciting Mary's death.*

### A DITTY

*These lines are from a resentful ditty which Queen Elizabeth*
*is said to have written about Mary, when the latter was a*
*" dangerous prisoner " in England. Puttenham in his "Arte of*
*English Poesie," says : " This was the action : our sovereign*
*lady, perceiving how by the Scottish Queen's residence within*
*this realm, at so great liberty and ease as were scarce worthy*
*of so great and dangerous a prisoner, bred secret factions among*

---

[1] This superstition really dates from the Roman days, and is referred
to by Ovid.

*her people, and made many of her nobility incline to favour her
party : to declare that she was nothin ignorant in those secret
favours, though she had long with great wisdom and patience
dissembled it."*

The daughter of debate, that eke discord doth sow,
Shall reap no gain where former rule hath taught still peace
to grow.
No foreign banished wight shall anchor in this port,
Our realm it brooks no stranger's force ; let him elsewhere
resort.
Our rusty sword with rest shall first his edge employ,
To *poll* their tops that seek such change, and gape for joy.

LETTER FROM SIR FRANCIS WALSINGHAM TO
SIR AMICE POULET, FEBRUARY 1, 1586

*The following letter expresses the displeasure of Queen
Elizabeth with Sir Amice Poulet, who, in 1585, succeeded Sir
Ralph Sadler in taking charge of the custody of the Scottish
Queen at Fotheringay.*

After our hearty commendations, we find by speech lately
uttered by Her Majesty, that she doth note in you both a lack
of that care and zeal of her service, that she looketh for at
your hands, in that you have not in all this time of yourselves
found out some way to shorten the life of that Queen Mary,
considering the great peril she is subject unto hourly, so long
as the said Queen shall live. Wherein besides a kind of lack
of love towards her, she noteth greatly that you have not that
care of your own particular safeties, that reason and policy
commandeth, especially having so good a warrant and
ground for the satisfaction of your consciences towards God,

78

and the discharge of your credit and reputation towards the world, as the Oath of Association, which you both have so solemnly taken and vowed, and especially the matter wherewith she standeth charged, being so clearly and manifestly proved against her. And therefore the Queen taketh it most unkindly that men professing that love towards her, that you do, should in any kind of sort, for lack of the discharge of your duties, cast the burden upon her, knowing, as you do, her indisposition to shed blood, especially of one of that sex and quality, and so near to her blood as the said Queen is. These respects we find do greatly trouble her Majesty, who, we assure you, has sundry times protested, that, if the regard of the danger of her good subjects and faithful servants did not more move her than her own peril, she would never be drawn to assent to the shedding of her blood. We thought it very meet to acquaint you with these speeches lately passed from her Majesty, referring the same to your good judgements, and so we commit you to the protection of the Almighty.

Your most assured friends,<br>
FRANCIS WALSINGHAM.<br>
WILLIAM DAVISON.

### REPLY FROM SIR AMICE POULET TO SIR FRANCIS WALSINGHAM, FEBRUARY 2, 1586

*This noble letter, which is all the more remarkable, because it must have been written spontaneously and with the greatest speed while the messenger waited, resembles the reply of the governor of a fortress to Charles IX., who had ordered him to massacre all the Protestants within his district. " Sire, j'ai communiqué vos ordres au garnison. J'y trouve loyaux sujets et braves soldats, mais point d'assassins."*

Your letters of yesterday coming to my hands this present day at five in the afternoon, I would not fail, according to your directions, to return my answer with all possible speed, which shall deliver unto you, with great grief and bitterness of mind, in that I am so unhappy to have lived to see this unhappy day, in the which I am required, by direction from my most gracious Sovereign to do an act, which God and the law forbiddeth. My good livings and life are at her Majesty's disposition and I am ready to lose them this next morrow, if it shall so please her, acknowledging that I hold them as of her most gracious favour, and do not desire them to enjoy them, but with her Highness's good liking. But God forbid, that I should make so foul a shipwreck of my conscience, or leave so great a blot to my posterity, to shed blood without law and warrant. Trusting that her Majesty of her accustomed clemency will take this my dutiful answer in good part (and rather by your good mediation) as proceeding from one, who will never be inferior to any Christian subject living in duty, honour, love and obedience towards his Sovreign. And thus I commit you to the mercy of the Almighty. From Fotheringay.

Your most assured poor friends,
A. Poulet.
D. Drury.
*Rawlinson MS., vol. 85, p. 89.*

REPORT OF THE WAY IN WHICH QUEEN MARY STUART OF SCOTLAND AND QUEEN DOUAIRIERE OF FRANCE WAS BEHEADED ON THE 18TH DAY OF FEBRUARY, 1587, IN THE CASTLE OF FOTHERINGHAY

Ὦ θάνατε Παιὰν, μόνος ἰατρὸς τῶν ἀνηκέστων κακῶν.—*Æschylus*.

And the execution therefore took place in this wise :

At the command of the Queen of England (through the secretary, Beale), the Earls of Shrewsbury and Kent, who were at the time in the neighbourhood of the castle of Fotheringhay, together with other gentlemen, knights and noble persons, with Sir Amias Paulet and Sir Drury, who had order to guard the Queen of Scotland, had on the previous day, namely the 17th day of February, made known to the imprisoned Queen the will of Her Majesty of England. Thereupon she made reply that she was prepared and had long awaited this. She inquired when the execution would take place. Although this was left to her own choice, she asked that it might take place at once, on the very next day, namely on the 18th day of February of the new calendar, on a Wednesday. She besought God's help thereto. At the same time as this notification there were laid before the Queen various apologies, namely that the kingdom of England and its Queen had been compelled to make such a decision.

Hence on the 18th day of February, at 7 o'clock of the morning, the aforementioned earls, knights and noblemen forgathered in the castle of Fotheringhay. Two followers were allocated to each knight, but only one to the others present, so that about eighty to a hundred persons entered the castle, beside the guard and the officials of the court.

There, in the large hall, in front of the fireplace, in which burnt a great fire, a dais had been set up, which was twelve feet wide and eight feet high. It was completely covered with black cloth, and thereon stood a chair with a cushion. As now all was ready, and the gentlemen had collected there between the hours of eight and nine, a message was sent to the imprisoned Queen that the gentlemen had come on the errand of which she had been forewarned in the afternoon of yesterday, and wished to know whether she were ready.

The messenger, however, found the door of her chamber locked and bolted. All her people were with her in the chamber. When the gentlemen heard this, they sent a messenger once more commanding him to knock at the door, should he not find it open, and to deliver the former message.

But he found the door unlocked. He sent one of the Queen's servants to her in order to acquaint her with his command. The servant brought answer that the Queen was not yet ready. After half an hour, the gentlemen sent to her once more, and thereto she made answer that she would be ready in half an hour.

After this time the chief official went to the Queen. He found her on her knees with her ladies-in-waiting, praying, and told her that her time was now come. Thereupon she stood up and said that she was ready. She was led between two men of her retinue into the antechamber. There she found all her people assembled. She exhorted them all to fear God and to live in humility of spirit. She took leave of them all, kissed the women and held out her hand to the men to kiss. She begged them not to grieve on her account but to be of good cheer and to pray for her. Then she was led to the stairway. There all the gentlemen advanced from the hall towards her, and the Earl of Shrewsbury said to the sorrowing Queen : " Madame, we are here to carry out the behest of our most gracious Queen of England, which was communicated unto you yesterday." The warrant and sentence the Earl of Kent held in his hand. The Great Seal of the Crown of England was thereon. Then the Queen replied that she would as lief die as live any longer. As she turned round she perceived her most distinguished servitor, Melville, and said to him : " My faithful servant Melville, though thou art a Protestant and I a Catholic, there is nevertheless but one Christendom and I am thy Queen, born and anointed, of the lineage of Henry VII. And so I adjure thee before God that thou give this command to my son : I beg him to serve God, and the Catholic Church, and to rule and keep his country in peace and to submit (as I have done) to no other Master, although I had the right good will to unite the kingdoms of this island. I renounce this, may he do likewise, and do not let him put overmuch trust in the presumption of the world. Let him trust God and then he will be blessed by Him. Let him speak no evil of the Queen of England, and thou, Melville, art my witness that I die like a true Scotswoman, Frenchwoman, and Catholic, which belief has ever been mine." These words and such like did she repeat.

Thereupon Melville made answer : " Most venerable and most august Princess, as I have been at all times your Majesty's faithful servant, so will I now with the help of God, faithfully and honestly transmit to the King, your Son, Your Majesty's words and message."

Thereupon she turned to the above-mentioned gentlemen and desired to have her priest with her on the dais, so that he might bear witness for her to the King of France and in other places, that she had died righteously and a good

G 2

Catholic. To this the gentlemen made reply that it had been ordained otherwise.

She then demanded that her servants might remain with her. This was refused, in order to curb her impatience and to free her mind from certain supersititions. Nevertheless five of her servants and two tiring-women were permitted to come to her, because she complained that she was being poorly served. She promised that she would cause no hindrance, either by cries or by tears. Further she demanded for her servants and her maids liberty to depart, with good escort, and free of cost to their own countries without let or hindrance. This the gentlemen promised her. Also that they should be permitted to retain everything that the Queen of Scotland had presented to them. But she repeated once more : " I desire that this take place." Thereupon she was led by two servants of the Governor to the dais. There she seated herself upon a chair, for she could stand but with difficulty. The earls seated themselves beside her. Then the Secretary Beale read the warrant and the sentence of execution in an over loud voice.

The gown in which the Queen was attired was of exquisite black velvet which she had likewise worn when she appeared before the gentlemen. In her hand she held a small cross of wood or of ivory with the picture of Christ thereon, and a book. On her neck hung a golden crucifix, and from her girdle a rosary.

Near her stood a doctor of theology, Dean of Peterborough, who, at the command of the gentlemen, spoke words of Christian comfort to her, exhorting her to die as a Christian with a repentant heart. She at once interrupted him and begged him to keep his peace, for she was fully prepared for death. The Dean answered that he had been commanded

to speak the truth to her. But she said for the second time :
" I will not listen to you, Mr. Dean. You have nought to do
with me. You disturb me." Thereupon he was bidden to
be silent by the gentlemen.

The Earl of Kent said to her : " Madame, I am grieved on
your account to hear of this superstition from you and to see
that which is in your hand. She said it was seemly that she
should hold the figure of Christ in her hand thereby to think
of Him. Thereupon he answered that she must have Christ
in her heart, and further said that though she made demur
in paying heed to the mercies vouchsafed to her by God
All-Highest, they would never-theless plead for her with
God Almighty, that He would forgive her sins and receive
her into His Kingdom. Thereto the Queen made reply :
" Pray, then will I also pray." Then the aforesaid Doctor
fell on his knees on the steps of the dais and read in an over
loud voice a fervent and godly prayer for her, most suitable
to such an occasion, also for the Queen of England and the
welfare of the Kingdom. All those standing round repeated
the prayer. But as long as it lasted the Queen was praying
in Latin and fairly audibly, holding the crucifix in her hand.

When the prayer was now ended on both sides, the
executioner knelt in front of the Queen. Him she forgave
his deed, as also all those who lusted after her blood, or
desired her death. She further forgave all and sundry and
craved from God that He might also forgive her own tres-
passes. Thereafter she fell on her knees in ardent supplica-
tion and besought the remission of her sins. She said that
she trusted to be saved through the death of Christ and His
Blood and that she was ready to have her own blood spilt at
His feet, wherefore she held His picture and the crucifix in
her hands. Further she prayed for a happy, long and

85

prosperous reign for the Queen of England, for the prosperity of the British Isles, for the afflicted Christian Church and the end of all misery. She also prayed for her son, the King of Scots, for his upright and honourable Government and of his conversion to the Catholic Faith. At the last she prayed that all the saints in heaven might intercede for her on this day, and that God of His great goodness might avert great plagues from this Island, forgive her her sins and receive her soul into His heavenly hand.

Thereupon she stood up and prepared herself for death. She doffed her jewels and her gown, with the help of two women. When the executioner wished to assist her, she said to him that it was not her wont to be disrobed in the presence of such a crowd, nor with the help of such hand-maidens. She herself took off her robe and pushed it down as far as the waist. The bodice of the underskirt was cut low and tied together at the back. She hastened to undo this.

Thereafter she kissed her ladies, commended them to God, and because one of them was weeping too loudly, she said to her : " Have I not told you that you should not weep ? Be comforted." To her she gave her hand, and bade her leave the dais. When she was thus prepared, she turned to her servitors, who were kneeling not far off, blessed them and made them to pray for her. Afterwards she fell on her knees with great courage, did not change colour, and like-wise gave no sign of fear. One of her tirewomen bound a kerchief before her eyes. As she knelt down she repeated the 70th Psalm : " *In te, Domine, speravi* . . ." When she had said this to the end, she, full of courage, bent down with her body and laid her head on the block, exclaiming : " In manus tuas, Domine, commendo spiritum meum." Then one of the executioners held down her hands, and the other

86

cut off her head with two strokes of the chopper. Thus ended her life.

The executioner took the head and showed it to the people, who cried : " God spare our Queen of England ! "

When the executioner held up the head, it fell in disarray so that it could be seen that her hair was quite grey and had been closely cropped.

Her raiment and other belongings were by command taken from the executioner, but he was promised their equivalent in money. Everything that had been sprinkled with her blood, also the garments of the executioner and other objects, were promptly taken away and washed. The planks of the dais, the black cloth and all else were thrown into the fire, at once, so that no superstitious practices could be carried on therewith.

Her body was carried out, embalmed and made ready for burial. Where this will take place is as yet unknown. Her servants and courtiers were instructed to abide there until her remains had been honourably laid to rest. She was four-and-forty years of age, and was the most beautiful princess of her time.

She had as first spouse, Francis II., King of France, after him Henry Stuart, the son of the Earl of Lennox, her cousin, a truly handsome young man, by whom she had issue James VI., King of Scotland. But after she had caused Henry Stuart to be murdered, she took in marriage the Earl of Bothwell, who was imprisoned in Denmark, lost his senses and there died.

After this execution had taken place, the portals of the castle remained shut, until Henry Talbot, son of the Earl of Shrewsbury, had been dispatched to the English Court. When, the other day, he brought the tidings to London, the citizens of this town lit bonfires on all sides and rang the bells, because they were rid of the danger in which they had lived so long. It looks as if the populace believed that a new era had begun in which they hope that all will remain at peace.

Described by SAMUEL TOMASCON, who was present at the happenings.

*From " The Fugger News-Letters " (John Lane, 1924).*

### THE FUNERAL OF MARY QUEEN OF SCOTS

On Sunday, being the thirtieth of July, 1587, in the twenty-ninth year of the reigne of Elizabeth the Queen's Majestie of England, there went from Peterborough Mr. Dethick, alias Garter Principall King of Armes, and five heralds, accompanyed with forty horse and men, to conduct the body of Mary late Queen of Scotts from Fotheringhay Castle in Northamptonshire to Peterborough aforesaid, which Queen had remayned prisoner in England    years ; having for that purpose brought a royal coach drawn by four horses, and covered with black velvet, richly sett forth with escocheons of the arms of Scotland, and little penons round aboute it ; the body being inclosed in lead, and the same coffined in wood, was brought down and reverently put into the coach, at which time the heralds put on their coats of arms, and bareheaded, with torches light, brought the same forth of the castle, about ten of the clock at night, and so conveyed it to Peterborough,    miles distant from Fotheringhay Castle ; whither being come about two of the clock on the Monday morning, the body was received most reverently at the minster dore of Peterborough by the bishop, dean, and chapter, and Clarenceux King of Armes, and, in the presence of the Scotts which came with the same, it was layd in a vault prepared for the same in the quire of the saide church on the south side, opposyte to the tombe of Queen Catherine, Dowager of Spayne, the first wife to King Henry the Eighth. The occasion why the body was forthwith layd into the vault,[1] and not borne in the solemnity, was, because it was so extreame heavy by reason of the lead, that the gentlemen could never endure to have carryed it with leasure in the solemne proceeding, and besides was feared that the sowder might ripp, and being very hott weather might be found some anoyance.

*From " The Accounts and Papers relating to Mary Queen of Scots " (Camden Society, 1866).*

## A TRAGICALL EPIGRAM UPON THE DEATH OF MARY QUEEN OF SCOTS

When doome of Peers and Judges fore-appointed,
By racking Lawes beyond all reach of reason,
Had unto death condemn'd a Queen anointed,
And found, (oh strange !) without allegiance, treason ;
The axe that should have done that execution,
Shunn'd to cut off a head that had beene crowned,

[1] James I. transferred his mother's body to Westminster Abbey in 1612. " At this time the corps of Queene Mary, late Queene of Scotland, was translated from Peterborough unto Saint Peter's Church in Westminster, beeing thither attended by the Lord Bishop of Coventry and Litchfield. And upon Thursday, the eight of October, the Lord Archbishop of Canterbury, the Lord Chancelor, the Lord Privy Seale, and the Earle of Worcester, and other noblemen, and the Bishop of Rochester and the Deane of Westminster, met the corps at Clearkenwell about sixe a clock in the evening, and from thence, with plenty of torchlights, brought the body of the sayd Queen unto the Chappell Royall at Westminster, and on the south side thereof it was there interred that night, where the King had builded a most royall Tombe for her, where she now resteth." (Stowe, ed. Howes, 1631, p. 1002.)

Our hangman lost his wonted resolution,
To quell a Queene of noblenesse so renowned,
Ah, is remorse in hangmen and in steele
When Peeres and Judges no remorse can feele?
Grant Lord, that in this noble Ile, a Queene
Without a head may never more be seene.

*Sir John Harrington* (1561–1612).

## SHAKESPEARE ON MARY QUEEN OF SCOTS

*Shakespeare being under the patronage of Queen Elizabeth, and knowing her jealousy, would not, of course, praise openly her rival Queen, but in the " Midsummer Night's Dream," composed in 1592, that is, five years after the execution of Mary, he wrote these beautiful lines, which may possibly have referred to her.*

" Thou rememberest
Since once I sat upon a promontory,
And heard a mermaid [1] on a dolphin's back
Uttering such dulcet and harmonious breath,
That the rude sea grew civil at her song ;
And certain stars shot madly from their spheres
To hear the sea-maid's music."—*Act II.* 1.

[1] *Mermaid and sea-maid*, that is, Mary ; *on the dolphins back*, she married the Dolphin or Dauphin of France ; *the rude sea grew civil*, the Scotch rebels ; *certain stars*, the Earl of Northumberland, the Earl of Westmorland, and the Duke of Norfolk ; *shot madly from their spheres*, that is, revolted from Queen Elizabeth, bewitched by the sea-maid's sweetness.

# PART III

Build your nest upon no tree here ; for ye see God hath
sold the forest to death. . . .

*Samuel Rutherford* (1600–1661).

Where be they that before us weren,
Houndës ledyng, and hawkës beren,
That hadde both fieldes and woods ?

*Old Song.*

Il n'y a poinct de grand jour qui ne vienne pas a Vêpres.

*Old Proverb.*

Wel-i-wa, shal hys hornes blaw,
Holy-rode this day ;
Now is he dede, and lieth low
Who was wont to blaw them aye.

*Anon.*

As for oure body, it shalbe very asshes that are quenched,
and oure soule shal vanish as the soft ayre. Oure life shall
passe awaye as the trace of a cloude.

*Miles Coverdale* (1488–1568).

91

# THE BORROWED DAYS

*There is an old proverb, mentioned by various writers, which represents March as borrowing certain days from April. These days being stormy, our forefathers endeavoured to account for this circumstance by pretending that March borrowed them so that he might extend his power a little longer. Those who are addicted to superstition will not lend anything upon these days for fear that the borrower should employ the article lent to him for purposes of witchcraft against the lender.*

> March said to Aperill
> I see three hoggs[1] upon the hill;
> But lend your first three days to me,
> And I'll be bound to gar them die.
> The first, it shall be wind and weet,
> The next, it shall be snaw and sleet,
> The third, it shall be sic a freeze,
> Shall gar the birds stick to the trees.
> But when the borrowed days were gane,
> The three silly hoggs came hirplin[2] hame.

*From " The Complaynt of Scotland " (1549).*

[1] Sheep.            [2] Limping.

OF THE WEIRDIS[1] GIVEN TO MAKBETH AND
BANQUHO

*The wild tale of Macbeth (fl.* 1040), *Maormar*[2] *of Moray,
and the weird sisters, which the genius of Shakespeare immortalised, is here given by John Ballenden, who translated it from
the Latin of Hector Boece, probably about* 1536. *It is interesting to compare it with the simple lines in Andrew of
Wyntoun's rhyming chronicle which is said to have been finished
about a hundred years earlier :*

> *He saw three wemen by gangand ;
> And these wemen then thowcht he
> Three weird Systers most like to be.
> The fyrst he heard say gangand by
> " Lo, yonder the Thane of Cromarty ! "
> The tother woman sayd agane,
> " Of Moray yonder I see thee Thayne ! "
> The Thyrd than sayd, " I see thee King ! "
> All this he heard in his dremying. . . .*

*Holinshed's version of this story was not published until*
1577.

Nocht lang after, happened ane uncouth and wonderful
thing, by which followed soon a great alteration in the
realme. By adventure, Makbeth and Banquho were passing
to Fores, where King Duncane happened to be for the time,

---

[1] Prediction.
[2] The Office of Maormars was hereditary. They existed as independent rulers of separate provinces, before either Northern or Southern
Picts were united under Kings. For the Pictish race, at the earliest
point where history catches a glimpse of it, does not seem to have acknowledged any one supreme ruler, either hereditary or elective. When
forced to combine against foreign invaders, they chose a powerful chief
to be their temporary leader in war. After the establishment of Kings in
Pictland, the Maormars continued to preside as King's Deputies over the
provinces which they had formerly ruled as independent chiefs.

and met by the gait three women, clothed in strange, and uncouth weed. They were judged, by the people, to be weird sisters. The first of them said to Makbeth, " Hale, Thane of Glammis ! " The second said, " Hale, Thane of Cawder ! " and the third said, " Hail, King of Scotland ! " Then said Banquho, " What women be ye, so unmercifull to me, and so favourable to my companion ? For ye give to him not only lands and great rents, but great lordships and kingdoms ; and give me nought." To this answered the first of the weird sisters : " We show more felicite appearing to thee than to him ; for though he happen to be a king, his empire shall end unhappily, and none of his blood shall after him succeed ; by contrary thou shalt never be king, but of thee shall come many kings, which with long progression shall rejoice the crown of Scotland." As soon as their words were said, they suddenly vanished out of sight. Makbeth, revolving all things as they were said by the weird sisters, began to covet the crown ; and yet he concluded to abide while he saw the time gaining thereto, firmly believing that the third weird should come, as the first two did before. But, his wife,[1] impatient of long tarry, as all women are (specially where they are desirous of any purpose), gave him great artation[2] to pursue the third weird, that she might become ane Queen : calling him oft times febil coward, and not desirous of honours ; since he dared not assaile the thing with manhood and courage. Makbeth, by persuasion of his wife, gathered his friends to a counsel at Innerness, where King Duncan happened to be for the time. And because he found sufficient opportunity, he slew King Duncane in the VII. year of his reign.

[1] Graoch, granddaughter of Kenneth IV.
[2] Instigation.

95

## THE GARDENER

*Was ever tale more cruel than that of the unhappy gardener, who, tempted by the " lily-tincture of her face," fell into an ecstasy, and, crazed with love, asked too much of a coldly beautiful lady. Some of the stanzas in this fragrant old poem suggest the " Garmont of Gude Ladeis," by Robert Henryson.*

The gardener stands in his bower door,
With a primrose in his hand,
And bye there cam a leal maiden,
As jimp[1] as a willow wand.

" O ladie can ye fancy me,
For to be my bride ;
Ye'se get a' the flowers in my garden,
To be to you a weed.[2]

The lily white shal be your smock,
It becomes your body best ;
Your head shal be baskt[3] wi' gilly-flower,
Wi' the primrose in your breast.

Your gown shal be the Sweet William ;
Your coat the camovine[4] ;
Your apron o' the sallads neat,
That taste baith sweet and fine.

Your hose shal be the brade kail-blade[5]
That is baith brade and lang ;
Narrow, narrow at the cute,[6]
And brade, brade at the brawn.

[1] Slender.
[3] Decked.
[5] Colewart.

[2] Garment.
[4] Camomile.
[6] Ankle.

Your gloves shal be the marigold,
All glittering to your hand,
Weel spread owre with the blaewort
That grows amang corn-land."

*O fare ye weil, young man, she says,*
*Fareweil, and I bid adieu ;*
*Sin ye've provided a weed for me*
*Amang the simmer flowers,*
*I will provide anither for you,*
*Amang the winter-showers.*

*The new fall'n snaw to be your smock,*
*It becomes your bodie best ;*
*Your head shal be wrapt wi' the eastern* [1] *wind,*
*And the cauld rain on your breast.*

## TO HIS MAISTRES

*Alexander Montgomerie (c. 1545–c. 1610), besides his famous " The Cherrie and the Slae " and " The Bankis of Helicon," wrote sonnets of great charm, several of which seem to be translated from Ronsard. He was in the service of the Regent Morton and James VI., and travelled extensively on the continent. In his later years he became devout, and published a metrical version of the psalms. The twenty-third is, perhaps, the most beautiful in the collection.*

So suete a kis yistrene fra thee I reft
    In bouing doun thy body on the bed,
That evin my lyfe within thy lippis I left.
    Sensyne [2] from thee my spirit wald neuer shed. [3]

---

[1] This grim idea may have been suggested by the winds which buffeted the souls of carnal sinners in Dante's Inferno.
    [2] Since then.                [3] Separate.

To folou thee it from my body fled,
And left my corps als cold as ony kie.[1]
Bot vhen the danger of my death I dred,[2]
To seik my spreit I sent my harte to thee ;
Bot it wes so inamored with thyn ee,
With thee it myndit lykuyse to remane.
So thou hes keepit captive all the thrie,
More glaid to byde then to returne agane.
Except thy breath thare places had suppleit,
Euen in thyn armes thair doutles had I deit.

## TO THÉ FOR ME

Suete Nichtingale in holene[3] grene that han[ts]
To sport thy-self, and speciall in the spring,
Thy chivring chirlis,[4] vhilks changinglie thou [chants,]
Maks all the roches round about thé ring ;
Vhilk slaiks my sorou, so to heir thé sing,
And lights my louing langour at the leist ;
Yit, tho thou sees not, sillie, saikles thing !
The piercing pykis brods [5] at thy bony breist.[6]
Euin so am I, by plesur lykuyis preist,[7]
In gritest danger vhair I most delyte.
Bot since thy song for shoring[8] hes not ceist
Suld feble I for feir my conqueis quyt[9] ?
Na, na,—I love thé, freshest Phœnix fair !
In beuty, birth, in bounty but compair.[10]

*Idem.*

---

[1] Key.                         [2] Feared.
[3] Holly.                       [4] Quivering trills.
[5] Thorns prick.                [6] Bonnie breast.
[7] Likewise tried.             [8] Threatening.
[9] My conquest (or object of conquest) quit.
[10] Without peer.

TEMPUS FUGIT

Tak time in time, or time be tint,[1]
For time will not remaine.

*From " The Cherrie and the Slae."  Idem.*

THE TWENTY THIRD PSCHALME

The Lord maist hie
I know will be
An herd [2] to me ;
I cannot lang have stress, nor stand in neid ;
He makes my lair
In fields maist fair,
Quhair I bot care,
Reposing at my pleasure, safety feid.
He sweetly me convoys,
Quhair naething me annoys,
But pleasure brings.
He brings my mynd
Fit to sic kynd,
That fors, or fears of foe cannot me grieve.
He does me leid,
In perfect freid,[3]
And for his name he never will me lieve.
Thoch I wald stray,
Ilk [4] day by day,
In deidly way,
Yet will I not dispair ; I fear none ill,
For quhy thy grace
In every place,
Does me embrace,

[1] Lost.                    [2] Shepherd.
[3] Peace.                   [4] Each.

99                                    H 2

Thy rod and shepherd's crook me comfort still.
In spite of foes
My tabil grows,
Thou balms my head with joy ;
My cup owerflows.
Kyndness and grace,
Mercy and peice,
Sall follow me for all my wretched days,
And me convoy,
To endless joy,
In heaven quhair I sall be with thee always.

*Idem.*

### OLD SCOTTISH PROVERB

*Quoted by Roger Ascham in his " Toxophilus " (1545) to prove that Englishmen were better archers than Scotchmen.*

Every Englysshe Archer beareth under his gyrdle XXIIII. Scottes.

### CHRIST DIED FOR THEE

*The following is part of a sermon on 2 Cor. 5 preached by Robert Rollock (c. 1555–1599), principal of the newly-founded University of Edinburgh.*

Will ye spier at (*ask*) men and women when they are lying bathing themselves in wickedness, if they will gang to Heaven.   They will answer : *yes, they will gang to Heaven or ever their feet be cold.* . . . But, vain loon, thou never knew Christ's purpose in dying for thee.   His purpose was that thou should be a new man, and thou should not live for thine own self, but for him.   And the end shall prove (and

100

if thou proceed so, living for thyself, and not for him who has died for thee,) that the death of Christ never had force in thee. . . . Therefore look if thou livest in Christ ; and if thou dost so, then assure thyself that Christ died for thee.

## A SUMMER DAY

*Alexander Hume (1560–1609), son of the Comptroller of Scotland, was born at Reidbras, and educated some say at St. Andrew's, and some at St. Mary's. Later he travelled in France ; on his return he became attached to the Court of James VI., and finally went into the Church, and was appointed rector or minister of Logie.*

O Perfect Light, which shaid [1] away
 The darkness from the light,
And set a ruler o'er the day,
 Another o'er the night—

Thy glory, when the day forth flies,
 More vively doth appear
Than at mid day unto our eyes
 The shining sun is clear.

The shadow of the earth anon
 Removes and drawis by,
While in the East, when it is gone,
 Appears a clearer sky.

Which soon perceive the little larks,
 The lapwing and the snipe,
And tune their songs, like Nature's clerks,
 O'er meadow, moor, and stripe. [2]

[1] For shaded.                    [2] Rill.

Our hemisphere is polisht clean,
    And lighten'd more and more,
While everything is clearly seen
    Which seemit dim before :

Except the glistening astres bright,
    Which all the night were clear,
Offuskit with a greater light
    No longer do appear.

The golden globe incontinent
    Sets up his shining head,
And o'er the earth and firmament
    Displays his beams abread.[1]

For joy the birds with boulden [2] throats,
    Against his visage sheen [3]
Take up their kindly musick notes
    In woods and gardens green.

The dew upon the tender crops,
    Like pearlis white and round,
Or like to melted silver drops,
    Refreshis all the ground.

The time so tranquil is and still
    That nowhere shall ye find,
Save on high and barren hill,
    An air of passing wind.

All trees and simples, great and small,
    That balmy leaf do bear,
Than they were painted on a wall
    No more they move or steir.[4]

[1] Abroad.                          [2] Emboldened.
[3] Shining.                         [4] Stir.

Calm is the deep and purple sea,
  Yea, smoother than the sand ;
The waves that weltering [1] wont to be
  Are stable like the land.

The cloggit [2] busy humming bees,
  That never think to drone,
On flowers and flourishes of trees
  Collect their liquor brown.

The Sun, most like a speedy post
  With ardent course ascends ;
The beauty of the heavenly host
  Up to our zenith tends.

The burning beams down from his face
  So fervently can beat,
That man and beast now seek a place
  To save them from the heat.

The herds beneath some leafy tree
  Amidst the flowers they lie ;
The stable ships upon the sea
  Tend up their sails to dry.

With gilded eyes and open wings
  The cock his courage shows ;
With claps of joy his breast he dings, [3]
  And twenty times he crows.

The dove with whistling wings so blue
  The winds can fast collect ;
Her purple pens turn many a hue
  Against the sun direct.

[1] Tumbling.                    [2] Clogged.
            [3] Beats.

103

Now noon is gone ; gone is midday,
　The heat doth slake at last ;
The sun descends down West away,
　For three of clock is past.

The rayons of the sun we see
　Diminish in their strength ;
The shade of every tower and tree
　Extendit is in length.

Great is the calm, for everywhere
　The wind is setting down ;
The reek [1] throws right up in the air
　From every tower and town.

The gloming comes ; the day is spent ;
　The sun goes out of sight ;
And painted is the occident
　With purple sanguine bright.

Our west horizon circular
　From time the sun be set
Is all with rubies, as it were,
　Or roses red o'erfret.

What pleasure then to walk and see,
　Endlong a river clear,
The perfect form of every tree
　Within the deep appear,

O then it were a seemly thing,
　While all is still and calm,
The praise of God to play and sing
　With cornet and with shalm !

[1] Smoke.

104

All labourers draw home at even,
And can to others say,
Thanks to the gracious God of Heaven,
Which sent this summer day.

### O HAPPIE DEATH

O happie death, to life the readie way,
The ende of greefe, and salve of sorrowes all ;
O pleasant sleepe, thy paines they are bot play ;
Thy cup is sweete, although it taste of gall.
Thou brings the bound and wretched out of thrall
Within the port sure from the stormie blast,
For after death na mischiefe may befall,
But wo, wan-chance, and perrels all are past.
Of kindelie death nane suld affraied be
But sich as hope for na felicitie.

*Idem.*

### THE WIFE WHO WOULD A WANTON BE

All night I clatter upon my creed,
Prayand to God that I were dead ;
Or else out of this world he [1] were :
Then should I see for some remeid.
*Wo worth marriage for evermair !*

Ye should hear tell (and *he* were gane)
That I should be a wanton ane.
To learn the law of lovis layr [2]
In our town like me should be nane.
*Wo worth marriage for evermair !*

[1] Her husband.          [2] Doctrine.

I should put on my russet gown,
My red kirtill, my hose of brown,
    And let them see my yellow hair
Under my kerchief hingand down.
    *Wo worth marriage for evermair !*

Lovers both should hear and see,
I should love them that would love me ;
    Their hearts for me should ne'er be sair :
But aye unweddit should I be.
    *Wo worth marriage for evermair !*

*Anon.*


## ON THE BIRTH OF JAMES VI.

*The following lines are said to have been written in old
Scottish characters on the wall of the room in Edinburgh Castle
where James VI. was born.*

Lord Jesu Chryst that crounit was with Thornse,
Preserve the Birth quhais Badgie [1] heir is borne,
And send hir sonne successione to Reigne stille,
Lang in this Realme, if that it be Thy Will ;
Als grant, O Lord, quhat ever of Hir proceed
Be to Thy Honer Glorie and Praise ; Sobied. [2]


## ENVOY

*James VI. of Scotland and I. of England, son of Mary
Queen of Scots and Lord Darnley, was born in 1561, and pro-
claimed King a year later, on his mother's forced abdication.
He began his serious studies at a young age, and wrote with some
bitterness on the margin of a book :  " They wald haiff me
learn Latin before I can speak Scots."   There is no doubt that*

[1] Body.                          [2] So be it.

*he was a brilliant scholar and a great lover of the Classics. All*
*through his life he gave up much time to reading, declaring that*
*if he were not a King, he would be a University man. His*
*letters to his sons are full of charm, and are to be found in the*
*" Miscellaneous State Papers " (1501–1726), Brit. Mus. He*
*took a keen interest in their education, and encouraged the*
*intellectual ability of the future Charles I. The Basilicon*
*Doron was universally admired during his life time, and—Bacon*
*tells us—" filled the whole realm with a good perfume of*
*incense," but his " Counterblast to Tobacco," published in 1616,*
*is his most entertaining book. The following Envoy belongs to*
*a lost poem addressed by James to his bride, the Princess Anne*
*of Denmark, whose journey to Scotland was delayed by winter*
*storms, 1598–1590.*

> Rejois thairfoir my half in all
> Sin honest causes bene the stay
> Of presense : hope that meete we sall
> With greater glaidnes one a day
> > I pray the lorde above
> > To send it to us soone
> > Fair weil will that be done
> > And after ay.
>
> What mortall man may live but hairt,
> As I do now, sic is my case,
> For now the haill [1] is from the pairt
> Devidit, ilk in divers place,
> > The seas are now the bar
> > Which makes us distant far
> > That we may soon win narr [2]
> > God grant us grace.

[1] Whole.      [2] *I.e.*, near.

Full many causes sure I have
Which do augment my no and caire
But one more special nor the leave [1]
When I do think what joy was there
    What gladness & what greeting
    At our long wishit meeting
    I cannot weill [2] on weitting [2]
    My cheikes declare.

And since how we so soone were sheed [3]
And lost oure lang desired joy :
O what mischance I never redd
That lovers had sic cause of noy—
    For other lovers usis
    The are to make excuses
    Of absence : thus abuses
    Them Venus boy—

But we endure farr greater skaith [4]
For only one of them has paine
But we alike are wounded both
And careful till we meet again
    O, absence cruel fa [5]
    Why workis thou us sic na
    And garris [6] true lovers sa
    Farr shedd remaine—

Thou absence gives me cause to feir
Lest she be harmed by some mischance
Thou absence garris me greive to heir
Some worde from her ; thou garris me pance [7]

[1] *I.e.*, rest.         [2] *I.e.*, well, unwetting.
[3] *I.e.*, sundered.    [4] *I.e.*, harm.
[5] *I.e.*, foe.          [6] *I.e.*, long.
       [7] *I.e.*, consider.

What may for to eschew
Their sorrows which renew
And whiles I change my hue
Whiles falls in trance.

*From " Lusus Reginus," Book I., MS.*

## ANNE OF DENMARK'S ARRIVAL IN EDIN-
## BURGH, MAY 19TH, 1590

Upon Tuisday, the 19th of May, the queene made her entrie in Edinburgh. She came by the south side of the toun, by the West Port, in a coache. A young boy descending in a globe, which opened, delivered certane keyes, with a Bible and a Psalme Booke. Mr. Johne Russell made an harangue in Latine, and the cannons of the castell were discharged. The nobles of Scotland and the Danish road before, and a traine of ladeis behind. The queene herself road in a coache drawin with eight hors, accompanied with the citicens in their gownes, and some of them careing a pale of purple velvet above the coache. At the strait of the Bow, Mr. Hercules Rollocke, Maister of the Grammar Schoole, made an oratioun. At the Butter Trone, there were some young weomen coastlie apparrelled, standing upon a scaffold, playing upon organs, and singing of musicians. Mr. Johne Craig's sonne, a young boy, had a short oratioun to her. At the Tolbuith were five youths, clothed in gentlewomen's apparell, one having a sword, another a ballance, the third a booke, the fourth a target, and other two with their signes, all representing Peace, Plentie, Policie, Justice, Liberallitie, and Temperance. Everie one expouned the significatioun of their owne signes. Therafter, the queene went into the kirk, and satt in the east end, in the loft, under a faire cannabie of velvet.  Mr. Robert Bruce made the sermoun, which being ended within halfe an houre, the queene is brought furth.  Comming by the Croce, they see there Bacchus drinking, and casting glasses, violers playing, and musicians singing.  At the Salt Trone was represented the king's genealogie ; and at the root of the tree a young boy made an oratioun in Latine.  At the port of the Nether Bow were represented the seven planets, and the weird givin in Latine ; and a faire jewell, of a great price, called the A, was givin to the queene.  All the day there went, before the honest men of the toun, twentie-foure youths clothed, some with cloth of silver, others with white taffetie, and golden chaines about their neckes, legges, and armes, and visoures on their faces, making them seeme Mores.  The fore staires were covered, with tapestrie or faire coverings.  Mr. Andrew Melvill made an oratioun to the ambassaders, to their great admiratioun. The king acknowledged that he had honoured him and his countrie that day, promised never to forgett it, and commanded to print it with all diligence

*David Calderwood* (1575–1650).

INSCRIPTION ON ROSEBURN HOUSE

Gif you enter at Christis door
Incline your ear unto ye poor.

1562.

A WITCHES' SABBATH

*Agnes Sampson, known as the " wise wife of Keith," on being tortured by the orders of James VI. in 1591, confessed*

110

*that she had been at a night meeting in North Berwick Church, and that :*

" The devil in man's likeness met her going out into the fields from her own house in Keith, between five and sax at even, being alone, and commanded her to be at North Berwick Kirk the next night. She passed there on horseback and lighted down at the kirkyard. A little before she came to it, about eleven hours at even, she and others danced alang the kirkyard ; Geilie Duncan playing to them on a trump,[1] John Fian *missalit* (masked) led all the rest, the said Agnes and her daughter followed next, and some others, in all about ane hundred persons, whereof sax were men, and all the rest women. The women first made their homage, then the men. The men turned nine times *withershins about (i.e.,* contrary to the course of the sun, that is from west to east). The witches then took hands and danced a reel to the music of Geilie Duncan's Jew's trump, singing the while—

' Cummer, go ye before, Cummer go ye,
Gif ye will not go before, Cummer let me.'

" John Fian touched the doors with his staff and they

[1] The indictment against John Fian, the schoolmaster of Salpans, was that he had entered into a compact with Satan to provoke a storm which would wreck the King's ship on its way to Oslo, by throwing an enchanted cat into the water. For this imaginary crime he was sentenced to be tortured to death and strangled " on a Saterdaie in the end of Januarie, 1591, in the Castle of Edinburgh, which did give the King a great and pleasurable satisfaction of mind." At this period Scotland was stirred by an extraordinary number of witch trials. In 1597 a crafty woman called Margaret Atkins, being threatened with torture, confessed herself guilty, but undertook to purge the country of witches if her life was spared. " For the reason whereby she could tell, as soon as she looked upon any, whether they were witches or not. In this she was so readily believed, that for the space of three or four months she was carried from town to town, to make discoveries of that kind. She accused many innocent women, and they were put to death. In the end she was found to be a mere deceiver."

opened ; he then with his breath blew in the lights, which were like muckle black candles sticking round the pulpit. The devil then started up in the pulpit, like ane muckle black man, and callit everyane by his or her name, and they answered ' Here, Master.' . . . On his command they openit up the graves, two within and ane without the kirk, and cut off the joints of the fingers, toes and knees of the dead, and partit them amang them, so that having ground them to a powder they might work mischief therewith. They also put to sea on the day James was expected back from Denmark with his bride, and threw a cat into the water, pronouncing at the same time an invocation to the devil. This was intended to raise such a storm that the vessel would be wrecked and the king drowned. The witches added that they asked the devil why could not work the king any evil. And the Prince of Darkness replied, ' Because he is such a good man, I have no power over him. He is my greatest enemy.' "

## LETTER FROM JAMES VI. TO QUEEN ELIZABETH

*An anxious and amorous missive, expressing anxiety for an acknowledgment of a poem sent by James to the Queen, as " ab incerto authore," and sending a sonnet inclosed. Whatever might be his dislike of Elizabeth, his interest in the succession to the English throne prevented him from showing it. I am unable to fix the date of this curious letter, nor have I been able to find a copy of the sonnet alluded to. I should conjecture it to have been written very late in the reign of Elizabeth.*

MADAME AND DEAREST SISTER.—Notwithstanding of my instant writting ane letter unto you, yet could I not satisfie my unrestfull and longing spreit, except be writting of this few lynes, quhilk, albeit thay do not satisfie it, yet thay do stay the unrest thairof, quhill the answer is returning of this present. Madame, I did send you befoire [1] . Since then, dame Cinthia hes oft renewed hir hornis, and innumerable tymes soupit with hir sister Thetis, and the bearer thairof returnit, and yet voyde of answer. I doubt not ye have red, how Cupidis dart is fyery callid because of the suddaine insnairing and restles burning thairafter. Quhat can I ellis judge, but that either ye had not receaved it, except the bearer returned with the contrary report, or ells that ye judge it not to be of me, because it is *incerto authore;* for quhilk cause I have inserted my name to the end of this sonnet heir inclosit. Yet, one way am I glad of the answers keiping up, because I hope nou for ane maire full, after the reeding also of thir presentis, and heiring this bearar dilate this purpose mair at large, according to my secreit thochtis ; for ye know deid lettiris cannot answer na questions ; thairfore, I most pray you, how unappeirant so ever the purpois be, to trust him in it, as weil as if I myself spake it unto you, face be face, quhilk I wish I micht, sen it is specially in any maner only for that purpose that I have sent him. Thus, not doubting of your courtesie, I committ you, madame and dearest sister, to Goddis holy protection, the day and dait as in the uther letter.

Your mair loving and affectionatt
brother and cousin then (I feir) yet ye beleve,

JAMES R.

*Thompson MS. P.* 59.

[1] Here is a space in the MS.

## LETTER FROM JAMES VI. TO THE LAIRD
## OF DUNDAS (1600)

*The following letter shows that when the larder at Holywood was somewhat empty, the King, being exceedingly poor, did not hesitate to ask his guests for the wherewithal to make a fine feast.*

Right traist friend, we grete you heartilie weel. The baptism of our dearest son being appointit at Holyrud-house upon the XXIII. of December instant, whereat some princes of France, strangers, with the specials of our nobility being invited to be present, necessar it is that great provisions, gude cheir and sic uther things necessar for decorations thereof be providit, whilks cannot be had without the help of sum of our lovand subjects, quhair of accounting you one of the specialis, we have thought good to request you effectuouslie to propyne (present) with vennysons, wyld meat, Brissil fowls (turkeys), capons and sic other provisions as are maist seasonable at that time and errand, to be sent into Holyrud-house upon the 22nd day of the said moneth of December instant and herewithal to invyte you to be present at that Solemnitie to take part of your awin gude cheir as you tender our honour and the honour of the country : Swa we commett you to God. From Lithgow, this 6th of Decemr. 1600

JAMES R.

### SONNET

Fra bank to bank, fra wood to wood I rin,
Ourhailit with my feeble fantasie ;
Like til a leaf that fallis from a tree,
Or til a reed ourblawin with the win'.

Twa gods guides me ; the ane of them is blin',[1]
Yea and a bairn brocht up in vanitie ;
The next a wife[2] ingenrit of the sea,
And lichter nor a dauphin with her fin.

Unhappy is the man for evermair
That tills the sand and sawis in the air ;
But twice unhappier is he, I lairn,
That feedis in his hairt a mad desire,
And follows on a woman thro the fire,
Led by a blind and techit by a bairn.

*Mark Alexander Boyd* (1563-1601).

## JAMES TO THE ENGLISH PARLIAMENT, MARCH 31, 1607.

This I must say for Scotland, and may truly vaunt it. Here I sit and govern it with my pen ; I write, and it is done ; and by a clerk of the council I govern Scotland now—which my ancestors could not do by the sword.

## THE SCOTTISH PEOPLE.

They christen without the cross, marry without the ring. . . . They keep no holy-days, nor acknowledge any saint but St. Andrew. . . . Their Sabbath exercise is a preaching in the forenoon, and a persecuting in the afternoon. . . . They think it impossible to lose the way to Heaven, if they can but leave Rome behind them.

To conclude, the men of old did no more wonder that the great Messias should be born in so poor a town as Bethlem in Judea, than I do wonder that so brave a prince as King James should be born in so stinking a town as Edinburgh in lousy Scotland.

*Sir Anthony Weldon,*
*(who accompanied James on his return to Scotland in* 1617).

[1] Eros.          [2] Venus.

**115**                    I 2

## INCONSTANCY REPROVED

I do confess thou 'rt smooth and fair,
  And I might have gone near to love thee,
Had I not found the slightest pray'r
  That lips could speak, had pow'r to move thee ;
    But I can let thee now alone,
    As worthy to be lov'd by none.

I do confess thou 'rt sweet ; yet find
  Thee such an unthrift of thy sweets,
Thy favours are but like the wind,
  Which kisseth everything it meets :
    And since thou canst love more than one,
    Thou 'rt worthy to be kiss'd by none.

The morning rose that untouch'd stands,
  Arm'd with her briars, how sweet she smells !
But pluck'd, and strain'd through ruder hands,
  Her sweets no longer with her dwells ;
    But scent and beauty both are gone,
    And leaves fall from her, one by one.

Such fate, ere long, will thee betide,
  When thou hast handled been awhile,
Like fair flow'rs to be thrown aside ;
  And thou shalt sigh, when I shall smile
    To see thy love to every one
    Hath brought thee to be lov'd by none.

*Sir Robert Ayton* (1570-1638).

## OLD SCOTTISH PROVERB

A wheen o' mickles mak's a muckle.[1]

## THE ARMADA CASTAWAYS IN FIFE

*In the following letter (quoted in " Edinburgh Amusement,"
1771), Mr. James Melvill, Minister of Kilrennie, describes a
surprise visit from the Spanish Armada to the East coast of
Scotland. Notwithstanding this fact, James VI. wrote to
Queen Elizabeth assuring her that " The Spanish flete never
entered within any roade or haven within my dominions nor
never came neere to any of my costes."*

The year 1588 is known in history for the providential
destruction of the Spanish Armada. The news of it had
been blazed about for a long time ; and this island had found
the fearfull effects of it, to the outer subversion both of kirk
and policie, if God had not watched wonderfully over the
same. Sometimes we wer told of their landing at Dunbar,
sometimes at St. Andrew's and in Tay, and now and then at
Aberdeen and Cromarty friths. Within two or three months
after the rising of the General Assembly that year, by break
of day, one of our baillies of Anstruther came to my bed-side,
but in afray, and told me that a shipful of Spaniards were
arrived in our harbour not to give mercy, but to ask it. I
got up, and, after assembling the honest men of the town,
we met in the Tolbooth, and, after agreeing to hear them,
there came to us a very reverend man, of big stature and
grace, of a stout countenance, and gray-haired. After much
and low courtesie, bowing with his face near the ground, and

[1] Mickle means little, and muckle much. This proverb may be derived
from the Greek of Hesiod :
" Εἰ γάρ κεν καὶ σμικρὸν ἐπὶ σμικρῷ καταθεῖο,
Καὶ θαμὰ τοῦτ' ἔρδοις, τάχα κεν μέγα καὶ το γένοιτο,"

touching my sleeve with his hand, he began his harangue in the Spanish tongue, whereof I understood the substance ; and being about to answer in Latin, he having a young man with him to be his interpreter, the youth repeated what the other had said in good English. The sum was, that King Philip his master had rigged out a navie and army to land in England, for just causes, and to be avenged of manie intollerable wrongs he had received from that nation ; but God, for their sins had been against them, and, by storm and weather, had driven their navy by the coast of England, and him with certain captains (being the commander of 20 hulks), upon an isle of Scotland, called Fair Isle, where they were shipwrecked ; and as many as had escaped the merciless seas and rocks, had for 6 or 7 weeks suffered great hunger and cold, till getting the bark they were in, they had sailed from Orkney and were come to their speciall friends and confederates, to kiss the King's Majestie's hands of Scotland, and to find relief thereby to himself, and the gentlemen captains whose conditions were for the present most miserable and pittiful.

I answered in short, that howbeit our friendship could not be very great, seeing they and their King were friends to the greatest enemy of Christ, the Pope of Rome, and our King and we defyed him ; yet nevertheless, they should know that we were moved by human compassion and Christians of a better religion than they ; for whereas our people resorting among them for lawful affairs of merchandize wer taken and cast into prison, and their bodies committed to cruel flaming fire for the cause of religion, yet they should find nothing among us but works of mercy and alms. I showed him that the baillies had granted him licence, with the captains to go to their lodgings for their refreshments, and with great courtesy he departed. That night the laird of Anstruther came, and accompanied by a good number of the neighbouring gentlemen gave the said general and captains presence, and entertained them humanly and suffered the soldiers to come ashore to the number of 260, for the most part young beardless men, silly, traiked and hungered. To them, for a day or two, the inhabitants gave kail, pottage and fish. My address to them was conform to the prophet Elisha to the King of Israel in Samaria : " Give them bread and water." The names of the commanders were Juan Comes de Medina, general of 20 hulks, Captain Petricio, Captain de Lagaretto, Captain de Lustera, Captain di Mauritio, and Segnor Sejano. Meantime, all the while my heart melted within me for thankfulness to God, when I remembered the pridefull and cruell nature of these people, and how they would have used us, in case they had landed with their force against us, and saw much of the wonderful works of God's mercie and justice in making us see the chief Commander of them making such courtesie to poor seamen, and their soldiers so abjectly to beg alms at our doors and on the streets. Meanwhile they knew not of the wreck of the rest, but supposed their army was safely returned, till one day I got in St. Andrews a private account of the wreck of the gallies, which when I told to the General, he cryed out for grief and bursted and gratt. This Commander when he returned to Spain showed great kindness to a ship of Anstruther, that was arrested at Cadiz. He rode court for her, and highly commended Scotland to his King. He took the Seamen to his house, and enquired for the laird of Anstruther, for the minister and his host, and sent many commendations home.

But we thank God that we had seen them among us in this sort.

Written on the 10th day of August in the last year of the age 1600.

### LANTERNE OF LOVE, AND LADY FAIR OF HUE

Lanterne of love, and lady fair of hue,
O, pearl of price, most precious and preclair,
O, daisy dulce,[1] gayest that ever grew,
Of every wight most sweet and singular,
O, flour delyce, most flouring and fair,
Unto this tale, sweet turtle, thou attend,
My thirlet[2] heart so low into despair,
Unto thy mercy I meekly me commend.
O, gem of joy, inionit in my heart,
O, plant of price, most pleasant and perfyte,
The right remede of all my panis smarte,
My spirit is reft to see thy cullour quite.
Devoid of woe, of sorrow and of sight,
Whose beauties all no heart may comprehend ;
My visage wan, O lady of delight,
Unto thy mercy I meekly me commend.

Since thou art she who has my heart in cure,
My hope, my heal, my weill and eik my woe.
Let me not serve, your humble servitor,
For but remede my heart will burst in two.
Now lady fair, my friend and eik my foe,
Whom on but dowt all virtue does depend,
My heart, and mynd, where e'er I ride or go
Unto thy mercy meekly I me commend.
*Bannatyne*[3] *M.S., Advocates' Library, Edinburgh.*

[1] *I.e.*, sweet.      [2] *I.e.*, pierced.
[3] During the plague in 1568, George Bannatyne, then a young man, occupied himself in his enforced retirement by copying out Scottish poems, thereby preserving valuable specimens of the makars of the day.

## WAS NOCHT GUD KING SOLOMON

Was nocht gud King Solomon
Ravished in sundry wise
With every lovely paragon
Glistening before his eyes ?
If this be true, true as it was, lady, lady,
Should I not serve you, allace, my fair lady.

When Paris was inamorit
Of Helena, dame beauteous speir,
Then Venus first him promisit
To venture on and nought to fear ;
What sturdy storms endurit he, lady, lady,
To win her love, or it would be, my deir lady.

Know ye not how Troilus
Wanderit and lost his joy,
With fates and fevers marvellous,
For Cresseid fair that dwelt in Troy ?
Till pity planted into her breast, lady, lady,
To sleep with him and grant him rest, my deir lady.

I reid sometime how venturous
Leander was his love to please,
Who swam the water perilous
Of Abedon [1] those surging seas,
To come to her there as he lay, lady, lady,
Where he was drownit by the way, my deir lady.

[1] Abydos.

121

Anaxarete[1] so beautiful
Whom Iphis did behold and see
With sighs and sobbis pitifall,
That paragon long wooit he ;
And when he could not win her so, lady, lady,
He went and hangit himself for wo, my deir lady.

If all these wichts of wirdiness[2]
Endurit sic pains to take,
With valiant deeds and sturdiness,
Inventering for their ladies' sake,
Why should not I, pure simple man, lady, lady,
Labour and serve you the best I can, my dear lady.

*Ibid.*

### GIF ME THY HEART

O man, rise up, and be not sweir,[3]
Prepare against this gude New Year.
My New Year gift thou has in store :
Since I am he that bought thee deir ;
*Gif me thy heart, I ask no more.*

Gif me thy heart, for I should have it,
It is my right, therefore I crave it :
To win the same I suffered sore ;
And now am ready to receive it ;
*Gif me thy heart, I ask no more.*

---

[1] Anaxarete of Salamis was changed into stone for despising the love of Iphis, who hung himself.—(Ovid, " Metamorphoses," xiv. 750.)
[2] Men of importance.　　　　　　　　　　[3] Lazy.

I have thee freed from all thirlage,
And have prepared thine heritage,
Where death shall never thee devoure :
And now am come to crave my wage ;
*Gif me thy heart, I ask no more.*

Since this last yeere thou hast offended,
Contrair my law they life hast spendit,
My mercy is ready now as before—
In this New Year all may be mended ;
*Gif me thy heart, I ask no more.*      *Ibid.*

### THUS SPAKE THE REEDS IN THE LOCH

Tho raging stormes move us to shake
And wind mak waters us o'erflow,
We yield thereto, but do not break,
And in the calm unbent we grow—
So, baneist [1] men, the princes rage,
And prisoners, be not despairit.
Abide the blast whill that it 'suage,
For time sic causis has repairit.      *Anon.*

### INSCRIPTION ON MARISCHAL COLLEGE, ABERDEEN, 1593 [2]

𝔗𝔥𝔢𝔶 𝔥𝔞𝔦𝔣 𝔰𝔞𝔦𝔡, 𝔔𝔲𝔥𝔞𝔱 𝔰𝔞𝔶 𝔱𝔥𝔞𝔶,
𝔏𝔞𝔱 𝔱𝔥𝔞𝔪𝔢 𝔰𝔞𝔶,

### IF YOU WOULD LUFE AND LUVIT BE

If you would lufe and luvit be,
In mynd keip weill these thingis three,

[1] Cursed.
[2] This motto of the Keiths, who from the twelfth century had held
the hereditary office of Great Marischal of Scotland, was first uttered

And sadly in thy breast imprent ;
*Be secret, true, and patient.*

For he that patience cannot leir [1]
He shall displeasance have perqueir,
Though he had all this worldis rent ;
*Be secret, true, and patient.*

For who that secret cannot be,
Him all good fellowship shall flee,
And credence none shall him be lent ;
*Be secret, true, and patient.*

And he that is of heart untrue,
Fra he be rend,[2] farewell, adieu,
Fie on him, fie, his fame is went ;
*Be secret, true, and patient.*

Thus he that wants of the things three
A lover glad may never be,
But ay is something discontent ;
*Be secret, true, and patient.*

Nocht with thy tongue thyself discure [3]
The things that thou hast of nature,
For if thou dois thou should repent ;
*Be secret, true, and patient.*                        *Anon.*

by George, fifth Earl (1553-1623) in defiance of certain comments on his
plunder of the Church. He was the great man of his time, stood proxy
for James I. at the latter's marriage with Anne of Denmark, and
founded the Marischal College, Aberdeen, in 1593, converting, for
that purpose, a monastery.    Compare the inscription with these lines :
          Λέγουσιν ἃ θέλουσιν.   λεγέτωσαν οὐ μελ[ε]ι μοι.
                συ φίλ[ε] με.   συμφερ[ε]ι σοι.
    " They say what likes them, let them say, I care not I,
        But love thou me ; 'tis good for thee ''   .  .  .
which is the favourite " posy " on rings found at Pompeii.
    [1] Learn.                                              [2] Leave him.
                        [3] Discourse.

                             124

## ANE SANG OF THE BIRTH OF CHRIST

*Angelus, ut opinor, loquitur*

*This is a translation of Luther's celebrated Christmas Carol,
" Von Himel hoch da kom ich her," written in* 1535 *for his
little son Hans.*

I come from Hevin to tell
The best nowellis that ever befell ;
To you this tythinges trew I bring,
And I will of them say and sing.

This day to you is borne ane Childe
Of Marie meike and Virgine mylde,
That blissit Bairne, bining and kynde,
Shall you rejoice baith heart and mynd.

My saul and lyfe, stand up and see
Who lyes in ane cribe of tree,
What Babe is that, so gude and faire ?
It is Christ, God's sonne and aire.

O, God ! that made all creature,
How art thow becum so pure,
That on the hay and straw will lye,
Amang the asses, oxen and kye ?

And were the world ten tymes so wide
Clad over with gold and stones of pride,
Unworthy yet it were to thee,
Under thy feet a stool to bee.

O, my deir heart, young Jesus sweit,
Prepare thy cradle in my spreit,
And I shall rocke thee in my hert,
And never mair from thee depart.

125

But I shall praise thee ever moir,
With sangs sweet unto thy gloir,
The knees of my heart shall I bow,
And sing that right Balulalow.

Gloir bee to God eternally,
Who gave his only Son for mee,
To come and save me from distress,
How can I thank his gentelnesse?

*From " Ane compendious Booke of Godly and spiri-*
*tuall Sangs, collectit out of sundrie partes of the*
*Scripture." Edinburgh, 1578.*


THE SOUL TO ITS REDEEMER

All my Lufe, leif me not,
  Leif me not, leif me not!
All my lufe, leif me not,
  Thus myne alone ;
With ane burden on my back,
I may not beir it I am sa waik,
Lufe, this burden from me tak,
  Or ellis I am gone.

With sinnis I am ladin sore,
  Leif me not, leif me not,
With sinnis I am ladin sore,
  Leif me not alone !
I pray thee, Lord, thairfoir,
Keip not my sinnis in stoir,
Loose me, or I be forloir,
  And hear my mone.

With thy handis thou hes me wrocht,
    Leif me not, leif me not !
With thy handis thou hes me wrocht,
    Lief me not alone !
I was sold, and thou me bocht,
With thy blude thou hes me coft,
Now am I hidder socht
    To thee, Lord, alone.

I cry and I call to thee
To leif me not, to leif me not,
I cry and I call to thee
    To leif me not alone.
All they that laden be,
Thou biddis thame come to thee ;
Then sall they savit be
    Throw thy mercy alone. . . .

Faith, Hope, and Charitie,
    Leif me not, leif me not !
Faith, Hope, and Charitie,
    Leif me not alone !
I pray thee, Lord, grant me
Thir godly giftis thrie,
Then sall I savit be,
    Doubt have I none. . . .

                                        *Ibid.*


### CHRIST TO THE SINNER

*Who is at my windo?  Who, who?*
*Go from my windo, go, go !*
*Who callis thair, sa lyke a strangeir ?*
    *Go from my windo, go !*

127

Lord, I am hair, ane wretchit mortall,
That for Thy mercy dois cry and call
Unto The, my lord celestiall.
    Se who is at my windo, who ? . . .

With richt humbill hart, lord, The I pray,
Thy comfort and grace obtain I may :
Schew me the path and reddy way
    In at Thy doore for to go . . .

*How dare thow for mercie crie,*
*Sa lang in sinne as thow dost lie ?*
*Mercie to have thow art not worthie,*
    *Go from my windo, go.*

Lord, I pray The with all my hart,
Of Thy greit mercy remuve my smart,
Let ane drop of Thy grace be my part,
    That in at Thy doore I may go . . .

*Remember thy sin, and als thy smart,*
*And als for the what was my part :*
*Remember the speir that thirlit my heart,*
    *And in at my doore thou sall go . . .*

*I ask na thing of the thairfoir,*
*But lufe for lufe, to lay in stoir :*
*Gif me thy hart, I ask no moir,*
    *And in at my doore thow sall go . . .*

*Who is at my windo ?   Who ?*
*Go from my windo, go !*
*Cry na mair thair, lyke ane stranger*
    *But in at my doore thow go.*

                                        *Ibid.*

## EDENBORROW

From Fishrawe, I rode the rest of the way, and so came to Edenborrow, seated in Lodoney [1] (of old called Pictland,) the most civill Region of Scotland being hilly and fruitful of corne, but having little or no wood. This City is the seat of the King of Scotland, and the Courts of Justice are held in the same. This City is high seated, in a fruitful soyle, and wholesome aire, and is adorned with many noblemen's Towers laying about it, and aboundeth with many springs of sweet waters. At the end towards the East, is the King's Pallace joyning to the Monastery of the Holy Crosse, which King David the first built, over which, in a Parke of Hares, Conies, and Deare, an high mountain hangs, called the chaire of Arthur. From the King's Pallace at the East, the City still riseth higher and higher towards the West, and consists especially of one broad and very faire street. [2] At the farthest end towards the West, is a very strong Castle, which the Scots hold unexpugnable—And from this Castle towards the West, is a most steep Rocke pointed on the highest top, out of which this Castle is cut : But on the North and South sides without the walls, lie plain and fruitful fields of Corne. In the midst of the foresaid faire street, the Cathedrall Church is built, which is large and lightsome, but little stately for the building, and nothing at all for the beauty and ornament.

*From " An Itinerary " (1617) by Fynes Moryson*
*(1566–1630).*

## AN APPRECIATION

Edinborough—The heart of Scotland, Britaine's other eye.

BEN JONSON (*c.* 1573–1637).

[1] *I.e.*, Lóthian.     [2] High Street and Canongate.

## THREE SONNETS

*William Alexander, Earl of Stirling (1567 ?–1640), Scottish courtier and poet, studied at Glasgow and Leyden, and travelled in France, Spain, and Italy. He received the Grant of Nova Scotia in 1621, and ten years later became the sole proprietor of King James's version of the psalms. Stirling was appointed Secretary for Scotland in 1626, but being a royalist and anti-Presbyterian he was unpopular and his last years were embittered. He died in 1640, insolvent, " old and extremely hated." Stirling wrote several tragedies. None of them show dramatic power, but they contain some fine lyrics.*

I

All that behold me on thy beauty's shelf,
To cast myself away, tossed with conceit,
Since thou wilt have no pity of my state,
Would that I took some pity of myself.
" For what," say they, " though she disdain to bow,
And takes a pleasure for to see thee sad,
Yet there be many a one that would be glad,
To boast themselves of such a one as thou."
But, ah, their counsel of small knowledge savours,
For, O, poor fools, they see not what I see,
Thy frowns are sweeter than their smiles can be,
The worst of thy disdains worth all their favours.
I rather, dear, of thine one look to have,
Than of another all that I would crave.

2

Small comfort might my banish'd hopes recall
When 'whiles my dainty fair I sighing see ;
If I could think that one were shed for me,
It were a guerdon great enough for all :

130

Or would she let one tear of pity fall
That seem'd dismiss'd from a remorseful eye,
I could content myself ungrieved to die,
And nothing might my constancy appall.
The only sound of that sweet word of " love,"
Press'd 'twixt those lips that do my doom contain,
—Were I embarked—might bring me back again
From death to life, and make me breathe and move.
 Strange cruelty ! that never can afford
 So much as once one sigh, one tear, one word !
*Idem.*

### 3

The love [1] Alexis did to Damon bear
Shall witness'd be to all the woods and plains
As singular, renown'd by neighbouring swains,
That to our relics time may trophies rear :
Those madrigals we sung amidst our flocks,
With garlands guarded from Apollo's beams,
On Ochills whiles, whiles near Bodotria's streams,
Are registrate by echoes in the rocks,
Of foreign shepherds bent to try the states,
Though I, world's guest, a vagabond do stray,
Thou mayst that store which I esteem survey,
As best acquainted with my soul's conceits :
 Whatever fate heavens have for me design'd,
 I trust thee with the treasure of my mind.

### MY LUTE

*William Drummond of Hawthornden* (1585–1649), *who
graduated at Edinburgh and studied law at Paris, was an*

[1] This sonnet was written to Drummond of Hawthornden, and is an
interesting testimony to the close friendship which subsisted between the
two poets.

131

*accomplished scholar and wrote exquisite sonnets and madrigals
formed upon the model of Petrarch and other Italian poets.
His prose meditations have some slight flavour of Sir Thomas
Browne. He enjoyed the friendship of Ben Jonson, and when
the latter paid his famous visit to " Classic Hawthornden " took
notes of his conversation which were long afterwards published.
Drummond was an ardent royalist, and sorrow at the execution
of Charles I. is supposed to have hastened his death. His
epitaph is composed of the last two lines of the beautiful sonnet
which he dedicated to his friend William Alexander, Earl of
Stirling : " Here Damon lies, whose songs did sometime grace
The murmuring Esk : may roses shade the place ! "*

My lute, be as thou wast when thou didst grow
With thy green mother in some shady grove,
When immelodious winds but made thee move,
And birds on thee their ramage [1] did bestow.
Sith that dear voice which did thy sounds approve,
Which us'd in such harmonious strains to flow,
Is reft from earth to tune those spheres above,
What art thou but a harbinger of woe ?
Thy pleasing notes be pleasing notes no more,
But orphan wailings to the fainting ear,
Each stop a sigh, each sound draws forth a tear :
Be therefore silent as in woods before,
   Or if that any hand to touch thee deign,
   Like widow'd turtle, still her loss complain.

### I KNOW THAT ALL BENEATH THE MOON DECAYS

I know that all beneath the moon decays,
And what by mortals in this world is brought,
In Time's great periods shall return to nought ;
That fairest states have fatal nights and days ;

[1] Warbling : Fr. *ramage.*

132

I know how all the Muse's heavenly lays,
With toil of spright which are so dearly bought,
As idle sounds, of few or none are sought,
And that nought lighter is than airy praise ;
I know frail beauty like the purple flower,
To which one morn oft birth and death affords ;
That love a jarring is of minds' accords,
Where sense and will invassal reason's power :
    Know what I list, this all can not me move,
    But that, O me ! I both must write and love.

*Idem.*

### FAIR IS MY YOKE

Fair is my yoke, though grievous be my pains,
Sweet are my wounds, although they deeply smart.
My bit is gold, though shortened be the reins,
My bondage brave, though I may not depart :
Although I burn, the fire which doth impart
Those flames, so sweet reviving force contains,
That, like Arabia's bird, my wasted heart,
Made quick by death, more lively still remains.
I joy, though oft my waking eyes spend tears,
I never want delight, even when I groan,
Best companied when most I am alone ;
A heaven of hopes I have midst hells of fears.
    Thus every way contentment strange I find,
    But most in her rare beauty, my rare mind.

*Idem.*

## ALEXIS, HERE SHE STAY'D

Alexis, here she stay'd ; among these pines,
Sweet hermitress, she did alone repair ;
Here did she spread the treasure of her hair,
More rich than that brought from the Colchian mines.
She set her by these musked eglantines,
The happy place the print seems yet to bear ;
Her voice did sweeten here thy sugar'd lines,
To which winds, trees, beasts, birds, did lend their ear.
Me here she first perceiv'd, and here a morn
Of bright carnations did o'erspread her face ;
Here did she sigh, here first my hopes were born,
And I first got a pledge of promis'd grace :
   But, ah ! what serv'd it to be happy so,
   Sith passed pleasures double but new woe ?

*Idem.*

## SLEEP

Sleep, Silence' child, sweet father of soft rest,
Prince, whose approach peace to all mortals brings,
Indifferent host to shepherds and to kings,
Sole comforter of minds with grief opprest ;
Lo, by thy charming rod all breathing things
Lie slumb'ring, with forgetfulness possest,
And yet o'er me to spread thy drowsy wings
Thou spares, alas ! who cannot be thy guest.
Since I am thine, O come, but with that face
To inward light which thou art wont to show,
With feigned solace ease a true-felt woe ;
Or if, deaf god, thou do deny that grace,
   Come as thou wilt, and what thou wilt bequeath,
   I long to kiss the image of my death.   *Idem.*

## THE BOOK OF THE WORLD

Of this fair volume which we World do name
If we the sheets and leaves could turn with care,
Of Him who it corrects and did it frame,
We clear might read the art and wisdom rare :
Find out His power which wildest powers doth tame,
His providence extending everywhere,
His justice which proud rebels doth not spare,
In every page, no period of the same.
But silly we, like foolish children, rest
Well pleased with coloured vellum, leaves of gold,
Fair dangling ribbands, leaving what is best,
On the great Writer's sense ne'er taking hold ;
    Or, if by chance we stay our minds on aught,
    It is some picture on the margin wrought.

*Idem.*

## OF A BEE

O ! do not kill that bee
That thus hath wounded thee !
Sweet, it was no respite,
But hue did him deceive,
For when thy lips did close,
He deemed them a rose.
What wouldst thou further crave ?
He wanting wit, and blinded with delight
Would fain have kiss'd, but mad with joy did bite.

## FROM THE "CYPRESS GROVE"

For to easy censure it would appear that the soul, if it can
fore-see that divorcement which it is to have from the body,

135

should not without great reason be thus overgrieved, and plunged in inconsolable and unaccustom'd sorrow : considering their near union, long familiarity and love, with the great change, pain, and ugliness, which are apprehended to be the inseparable attendants of death.

They had their being together, parts they are of one reasonable creature, the harming of the one is the weakening of the working of the other. What sweet contentments doth the soul enjoy by the senses ? They are the gates and windows of its knowledge, the organs of its delight. If it be tedious to an excellent player on the lute to abide but a few months the want of one, how much more the being without such noble tools and engines be painful to the soul ? And if two pilgrims which have wandred some few miles together, have a hearts-grief when they are near to part, what must the sorrow be at parting of two so loving friends and never-loathing lovers as are the body and soul ?

Death is the violent estranger of acquaintance, the eternal divorcer of marriage, the ravisher of the children from the parents, the stealer of parents from their children, the interrer of fame, the sole cause of forgetfulness, by which the living talk of those gone away as of so many shadows or age-worn stories : all strength by it is enfeebled, beauty turned into deformity and rottenness, honour into contempt, glory into baseness. It is the reasonless breaker off of all actions, by which we enjoy no more the sweet pleasures of earth, nor contemplate the stately revolutions of the heavens. The sun perpetually setteth, stars never rise unto us : it in one moment robbeth us of what with so great toil and care in many years we have heaped together : by this are successions of linages cut short, kingdoms left heirless, and greatest states orphaned : it is not overcome by pride, soothed by flattery, tam'd by intreaties, brib'd by benefits, softned by lamentations, nor diverted by time. Wisdom, save this, can prevent and help every thing. By death we are exiled from this fair city of the world, it is no more a world unto us, nor we any more a people unto it. The ruines of phanes, palaces, and other magnificent frames, yield a sad prospect to the soul, and how should it without horror view the wrack of such a wonderful masterpiece as is the body?

*Idem.*

## THREE METRICAL PSALMS

*Sir William Mure* (1594–1657) " *pious and learned, had ane excellent vaine in poyesie.*" *He translated Virgil, published miscellaneous poems, and left a fine paraphrase of the Psalms of which he himself says :* " *It is not to be presumed that this version, in the first draught, attained the intendit perfection. Let the reader observe and comport with this essay, till the Lord furnishing greater measure of light and better convenience of tyme, they be amendit.*"

I

The man is blessed verilie
    Who walketh not astray
In counsell of ungodlie men,
    Nor stands in sinners' way,
Nor sitts in scorners' seat, but setts
On God's law his delight,
And stedfastlie his law doth minde
    And muse on, day and night.

137

Hee shall be like unto the tree
　　Sett by the river side,
In seasoun due which fruit brings forth,
　　Whose leaves ay blooming bide.
His workes shall prosper all ; not so
　　Ungodlie men, for they
Shall be like chaffe, which stormie wynds
　　Sweep suddenlie away.

In judgment therefore shall not stand
　　Men wicked and profane,
Nor sinners, where the righteous flock
　　Assembled do remaine,
For, who so righteous paths persue,
　　The Lord doth know their way ;
But perrish shall the way of sin,
　　Wherein the wicked stray.


### XLV

Great thoughts for matter hath my hart
　　Digested ; I do sing
A work of weightie argument,
　　A poeme to the king.
My tongue is, (for enditeing prompt,)
　　As speedie writer's pen.
In beautie much more excellent.
　　Thow art then sonns of men.

Grace in thy lips diffused is ;
　　For ever therefor blest
Of God thow art.　Gird on thy thigh
　　Thy sword, thow Mightiest,

Thy glorie and thy majestie.
In majestie O ride
Most prosperouslie, for that the raines
Truth, meekness, justice guide.

Thy right hand terrors shall thee teach,
Thy Shaftis their wings shall steep
In hearts of the king's enemies,
And low the people keep.
Thy throne eternall is, (O God) ;
With equitie thow sweyes
Thy scepter. Righteousnes thow lovst,
And hatst all wicked wayes.

God therefor, evin thy God, the oyle
Of Gladnes on thy head,
Aboundantlie, above thy mates,
Hath, (not by measure,) shed.
Thy roabs of myrrhe, of aloes all,
And cassia sweetlie smell,
From Ivorie palaces, and theirs
That mak the glad excell.

Amongst thy weemen, honored most
By thee, kings' daughters stand.
The Queen, in Gold of Ophir clad,
Taks place at thy richt hand.
Advert and weigh, thine eare encline,
O Daughter ; whollie sett
Thyselff, thy freends, thy father's house,
Thy people to forgett.

Thus, in thy beautie shall the king
 Exceedinglie delight.
Thy Lord he is, to Him bow down,
 His honour is by right.
The daughter of renowned Tyre ;
 Of people not a few,
Who mightie are, with presents rich,
 Shall for thy favor sue.

All glorie inwardlie arrayes
 The daughter of the king ;
Roabs wrought on grounds of gold, around
 Her decentlie do hing.
In rare embroideries, to the king
 Shee shall be led along ;
(Her follow virgins after,) Shee
 To thee shall lead the throng.

They with rejoiceing shall bee brought
 With mirth and gladness great,
And, in the palace of the king,
 Shall be receavd with state.
Thy fruitfull ofspring shall the rooms
 Of sleeping fathers fill,
In all the earth, who shall derive
 From Thee dominion still.

My song to all succeeding times
 Thy name shall famous make ;
For ever, (therefore,) people shall
 Thy praise for subject take.

### CXVII

Praise yee Jehovah, nations all ;
All people laud the Lord ;
For plentifullie towards us
Hee mercy doth afford.
Exceeding great his kyndness is ;
No time his treuth doth bound.
Yee nations, yee, his people all,
Loud Halelujahs sound.

### SONNET TO MARGARET

Adieu ! my love, my life, my bliss, my being,
My hope, my hap, my joy, my all, adieu !
Adieu ! sweet subject of my pleasant dying,
And most delightful object of my view.
Bright spark of beauty, paragon'd by few ;
Unspotted pearle, which doth thy sex adorne ;
Loadstar of love, whose pure vermilion hew
Makes pale the rose and stains the blushing morne ;
That zeale to thee which I have ever borne,
Sole essence, lyfe and vigour of my spreit,
By tract of tyme shall never be outworn ;
My second self, my charming sweet.
And so, my Phœnix and my turtle true,
A thousand, thousand tymes adieu ! adieu !

*Idem.*

### THE WHALE

God's might so peopled hath the sea
With fish of divers sort,
That men therein may clearly see
Great things for their comfort.

141

There is such great varietie,
  Of fishes of all kind,
That it were great impietie
  God's hand there not to find.

The Puffen Torteuse, and Thorneback,
  The Scillop and the Goujeon,
The Shrimpe, the Spit-fish, and the Sprat,
  The Stock-fish, and the Sturgeon ;

The Torteuse, Tench, and Tunnyfish,
  The Sparling and the Trout ;
And Herring, for the poor man's dish,
  Is all the land about ;

The Groundling, Gilt-head, and the Crab,
  The Gurnard, Cockle, Oyster,
The Cramp-fish and als the Sea-Dog,
  The Crefish and the Conger ;

The Periwinkle and Twinfish—
  It's hard to count them all ;
Some are for oyle, some for the dish ;
  The greatest is the Whale !

                    *Zachary Boyd* (1585–1653).


FROM " GARGANTUA AND PANTAGRUEL "

Now is it that the mindes of men are qualified with all
manner of discipline, and the old sciences revived, which for
many ages were extinct : now it is, that the learned languages
are to their pristine purity restored, viz. Greek (without
which a man may be ashamed to account himself a scholar),
Hebrew, Arabick, Chaldaean and Latine. Printing likewise
is now in use, so elegant, and so correct, that better cannot

be imagined, although it was found out but in my time by divine inspiration, as by a diabolical suggestion on the other side was the invention of Ordnance. All the world is full of knowing men, of most learned Schoolmasters, and vast Libraries : and it appears to me as a truth, that neither in Plato's time, nor Cicero's, nor Papinian's, there was ever such conveniency for studying, as we see at this day there is : nor must any adventure henceforward to come in publick, or present himself in company, that hath not been pretty well polished in the shop of Minerva : I see robbers, hangmen, free-booters, tapsters, ostlers, and such like, of the very rubbish of the people, more learned now, then the Doctors and Preachers were in my time.

What shall I say ? the very women and children have aspired to this praise and celestial Manna of good learning.

*Translated from Rabelais by Sir Thomas Urquhart*
*(1611–1660).*

## LETTER FROM CHARLES I. TO HENRY PRINCE OF WALES (1611)

*The following boyish note from Charles I. to his brother Henry, Prince of Wales, whose death in 1612 left him heir to the throne, expresses the essentially human side of the writer.*

SWEET, SWEET BROTHER,

I thank you for your letter. I will keep it better than all my graith [1] ; and I will send my pistols by Master Newton. I will give anything that I have to you ; both my horses, and my books, and my crossbows, or anything that

---

[1] Possessions.

you would have. Good brother, love me, and I shall ever
love and serve you.

Your loving brother to be, commanded,

YORK.

## ON A QUIET CONSCIENCE

Close thine eyes, and sleep secure ;
Thy soul is safe, thy body sure.
He that guards thee, he that keeps,
Never slumbers, never sleeps.
A quiet conscience in the breast
Has only peace, has only rest.
The wisest and the mirth of kings
Are out of tune unless she sings :
Then close thine eyes in peace and sleep secure,
No sleep so sweet as thine, no rest so sure.

*Charles I.*

## THREE SUN-DIAL MOTTOES

### I

*In the King's garden, Holyrood, on the dial presented by
Charles I. to Queen Henrietta Maria.*

UNITED . IN . TIME . PARTED . IN

TIME . TO . BE . REUNITED

WHEN . TIME . SHALL . BE

NO . MORE.

### II

*At Liberton House*

As the sun runes
So Death comes.

1660.

## III

*At St. Anne's Court, Dunbar*
Watch, for ye kno not the houre.
1662.

### A DEER-HUNT IN BRAEMAR IN 1618

*The following deer-hunt was witnessed by John Taylor (1580–1653), the English " Water-poet," when he made an excursion on foot into the north of Scotland to pay a visit to the Earl of Mar at Braemar.*

Once in the year, which is the whole month of August, and sometimes part of September, many of the nobility and gentry of the kingdom, for their pleasure, do come into these Highland countries to hunt, when they do conform themselves to the habit of the Highlandmen, who for the most part speak nothing but Irish, and in former times were those people which were called the *Red-shanks*. Their habit is shoes with but one sole apiece, stockings (which they call short hose) made of a warm stuff of divers colours, which they call tartan. As for breeches, many of them, nor their forefathers, never wore any, but a jerkin of the same stuff that their hose is of, their garters being bands or wreaths of hay or straw, with a plaid about their shoulders, which is a mantle of divers colours, of much finer and lighter stuff than their hose, with blue flat caps on their head, a handkerchief knit with two knots about their neck, and thus are they attired. Now, their weapons are long bows and forked arrows, swords and targets, harquebusses, muskets, dirks, and Lochaber axes.

My good lord of Mar having put me into that shape

[costume], I rode with him from his house, where I saw the ruins of an old castle, called the castle of Kindroghit [Castleton]. It was built by king Malcolm Canmore for a hunting-house : it was the last house I saw in those parts ; for I was the space of twelve days after before I saw either house, corn-field, or habitation for any creature but deer, wild horses, wolves, and such-like creatures, which made me doubt that I should ever have seen a house again.

Thus the first day we travelled eight miles, where there were small cottages built on purpose to lodge in, which they call *lonchards*. I thank my good Lord Erskine, he commanded that I should always be lodged in his lodging, the kitchen being always on the side of a bank, many kettles and pots boiling, and many spits turning and winding, with a great variety of cheer—as venison ; baked, sodden, roast, and stewed beef ; mutton, goats, kid, hares, fresh salmon, pigeons, hens, capons, chickens, partridge, moor-coots, heath-cocks, capercailzies, and termagants [ptarmigans] ; good ale, sack, white and claret, tent [Alicante], with most potent *Aqua-vitæ*.

All these and more than these we had continually in superfluous abundance, caught by Falconers, Fowlers, Fishers, and brought by my Lord's tenants and purveyors to victual our Camp, which consisted of fourteen or fifteen hundred men and horses. The manner of the hunting is this : five or six hundred men do rise early in the morning, and do disperse themselves divers ways, and seven or eight miles' compass ; they do bring or chase in the deer in many herds (two, three, or four hundred in a herd) to such or such a place as the Nobleman shall appoint them ; then when day is come, the Lords and gentlemen of their companies do ride or go to the said places, sometimes wading up to their

146

middles through bournes and rivers ; and then, they being come to the place, do lie down on the ground, till those fore-said scouts, which are called the Tinchel, do bring down the deer. . . . Then, after we had stayed three hours or thereabouts, we might perceive the deer appear on the hills round about us (their heads making a show like a wood), which, being followed close by the Tinchel, are chased down into the valley where we lay. Then all the valley on each side being waylaid with a hundred couple of strong Irish greyhounds, they are let loose as the occasion serves upon the herd of deer, so that, with dogs, guns, arrows, dirks, and daggers, in the space of two hours, fourscore fat deer were slain, which after are disposed of some one way and some another, twenty and thirty miles, and more than enough left for us to make merry withal at our rendezvous.

## BONNIE GEORGE CAMPBELL

*This spirited little song is said to refer to the death of one of the adherents of the house of Argyll, who fell in the battle of Glenlivat in* 1594.

Hie upon Hielands
And low upon Tay,
Bonnie George Campbell
Rade out on a day.

Saddled and bridled
And gallant rade he ;
Hame came his gude horse,
But never cam he !

Out cam his auld mither
    Greeting fu' sair,
And out cam his bonnie bride
    Rivin' her hair.

Saddled and bridled
    And booted rade he ;
Toom [1] hame cam the saddle,
    But never cam he !

" My meadow lies green,
    And my corn is unshorn ;
My barn is to big,
    And my babie's unborn."

Saddled and bridled
    And booted rode he,
A plume in his helmet,
    A sword at his knee.

But toom cam his saddle
    All bluidy to see ;
Oh, hame cam his guid horse,
    But never cam he.


FRAGMENT

I wish I had died my own fair death,
    In tender age, when I was young ;
I would never [then] have broke my heart
    For the love of any churl's son. . . .

[1] Empty.

148

## WHEN I LIE WAKING ALL ALONE

Yestreen I made my bed fu' braid,
This night I'll mak' it narrow . . .
For a' the lee-lang winter night
I lie twined o' my marrow.[1]

## FRAGMENTS FROM THE LETTERS OF SAMUEL RUTHERFORD TO THE COUNTESS OF KENMURE

*Samuel Rutherford (1600–1661) took his M.A. at Edinburgh in 1621, and was appointed Professor of Humanity shortly afterwards. His correspondence with his godly friends has been called, not without reason, " the most seraphic book in our literature."*

### 1628

Ye have lost a child : nay, she is not lost to you who is found to Christ. She is not sent away, but only sent before, like unto a star, which going out of our sight doth not die and evanish, but shineth in another hemisphere. Ye see her not, yet she doth shine in another country. If her glass was but a short hour, what she wanteth of time that she hath gotten of eternity ; and ye have to rejoice that ye have now some plenishing up in heaven. Build your nest upon no tree here ; for ye see God hath sold the forest to death ; and every tree whereupon we would rest is ready to be cut down, to the end we may fly and mount up, and build upon the Rock, and dwell in the holes of the Rock. . . .

[1] Separated from her lover.

### 1630

It is God's mercy to you, madam, that He giveth you your fill, even to loathing, of this bitter world, that ye may willingly leave it, and, like a full and satisfied banqueter, long for the drawing of the table. And at last, having trampled under your feet all the pleasures that are under sun and moon, and having rejoiced as though ye rejoiced not, and having bought as though ye possessed not, ye may, like an old crazy ship, arrive at our Lord's harbour, and be made welcome, as one of those who have ever had one foot loose from the earth, longing for that place where your soul shall feast and banquet for ever and ever upon a glorious sight of the incomprehensible Trinity, and where ye shall see the fair face of the man Christ, even the beautiful face that was once for your cause more marred than any of the visages of the sons of men. . . .

### 1631

Madam, tire not, weary not ; I dare find you the Son of God caution, when ye are got thither, and have cast your eyes to view the golden city, and the fair and never-withering Tree of Life, that beareth twelve manner of fruits every month, ye shall then say, " Four-and-twenty hours' abode in this place is worth threescore and ten years' sorrow upon earth." . . .

#### THOU SHALT NOT STEAL

This book is mine, and if ye steal it away,
Remember at the Latter Day
Our Lord shall come to ye and say,
" Where is the book ye stole away ? "

*Written on a MS. book of accounts belonging to*
*Hew Love, 1601.*

## O WALY, WALY

*Although the girl in this unforgettable fragment varies her sorrow with reminiscences of her proud appearance in " cramoisie," the spell of poetic dignity and beauty is never broken. She had known some little joy, it seems, some lazy state ; but her mirthful days had been brief. So, far removed from " blanched linen smooth and lavendered," or soft matted floor, she goes to her naked bed on the cold unsheltered hillside, with only the quiet moon for company. " And all the world is bitter as a tear." . . .*

O waly, waly up the bank,
    And waly, waly down the brae,
And waly, waly yon burn-side
    Where I and my love wont to gae.
I lean'd my back unto an aik,
    I thought it was a trusty tree ;
But first it bow'd, and syne it brake :
    Sae my true love did lightly me.

O waly, waly gin love be bonny,
    A little while when it is new ;
But when it's auld, it waxes cauld
    And wears awa' like morning dew.
O wherefore should I busk [1] my head ?
    Or wherefore should I kame my hair ?
For my true love has me forsook,
    And says he'll never love me mair.

Now Arthur-seat shall be my bed,
    The sheets shall ne'er be 'filed [2] by me,
Saint Anton's [3] well shall be my drink,
    Since my true love has forsaken me.

[1] Wreathe.                      [2] Defiled.
[2] The well of Saint Anthony dates from about 1430.

*Martinmas wind, when wilt thou blaw,*
*And shake the green leaves off the tree?*
*O gentle death, when wilt thou come?*
*For of my life I am wearie.*

'Tis not the frost that freezes fell,
  Nor blawing snaw's inclemencie ;
'Tis not sic cauld that makes me cry,
  But my love's heart grown cauld to me.
When we cam' in by Glasgow toun,
  We were a comely sight to see ;
My love was clad i' the black velvet,
  And I mysell in cramoisie.

But had I wist before I kiss'd
  That love had been sae ill to win,
I had lock'd my heart in a case of gowd
  And pin'd it wi' a silver pin.
Oh, oh ! if my young babe were born,
  And set upon the nurse's knee ;
And I mysell were dead and gone—
  For a maid again I'll never be.

*From " The Tea-Table Miscellany," edited*
*by A. Ramsay* (1724).

# PART IV

The gardens of the Muses keep the privilege of the golden age ; they ever flourish and are in league with time. The monuments of wit survive the monuments of power : the verses of a poet endure without a syllable lost, while states and empires pass many periods.

*Francis Bacon, Lord Verulam.*

Poesy subsisteth by herself, and after one demeanour and continuance her beauty appeareth to all ages. In vain have some men of late, transformers of everything, consulted upon her reformation, and endeavoured to abstract her to metaphysical and scholastic quiddities, denuding her of her own habits, and those ornaments with which she hath amused the world some thousand years. Poesy is not a thing that is yet in the finding and search, or which may be otherwise found out.

*Drummond of Hawthornden.*

The aim of true poetry is to console the afflicted ; to add sunshine to daylight by making the happy happier ; to teach the young and the gracious of every age to see, to think, and to feel.

*Wordsworth.*

Tu n'expliques rien, ô poête, mais toutes choses par toi nous deviennent explicables.

*Paul Claudel.*

153

*This reminds us of the old English prophecy, " When hempe is spun England is done," which Lord Bacon heard when he was a child and interpreted as follows : Hempe is composed of the initial letters of Henry, Edward, Mary, Philip, and Elizabeth. At the close of the last reign " England was done," for the sovereign no longer styled himself " King of England," but " King of Great Britain and Ireland."*

When HEMPE is come and also gone,
SCOTLAND & ENGLAND shall be all one.

| K | K | Q | K | Q |
|---|---|---|---|---|
| HENRY | EDWARD | MARY. | PHILIP | ELIZABETH. |
| the 6. | the 6. | | of Spain, M. Husb. | |

H    E    M    P    E

Praised be God alon, for HEMPE is cum & gon
And left vs old Albion, by peace joyned in one.

SIX SELECTIONS FROM THE "COMMENTARY UPON THE FIRST EPISTLE OF ST. PETER"

*Robert Leighton (1611-1684), Archbishop of Glasgow, was a noted Scottish divine, who aimed to preserve what was best in Episcopacy and Presbytery as a basis for comprehensive union. His works show a deep spirituality.  Bishop Burnet, who knew him well, said that " his preaching had a sublimity both of thought and expression. . . . There was a majesty and beauty in it that I cannot yet forget. . . ."*

## Sacrifice

Stay not away because thou, and the gifts thou offerest, are inferior to the offering of others.  No, none are excluded for that; only give what thou hast, and act with affection, for that he regards most.  Under the law, they who had not a lamb, were welcome with a pair of pigeons.  So that the Christian may say, " What I am, Lord, I offer myself unto Thee, to be wholly Thine : and had I a thousand times more of estate, or wit, or learning, or power, I would endeavour to serve Thee with all.  What I have, I offer Thee, and it is most truly Thine ; it is but of Thy own that I give Thee."  No one needs forbear sacrifice for poverty, for what God desires, is the heart, and there is none so poor, but hath a heart to give him.

## Instability

The doubled-minded man (says St. James) is unstable in all his ways.  Although the word usually signifies deceitfulness and dissimulation of mind—answering to the Hebrew phrase, " a heart and a heart,"—yet here I conceive it hath

another sense ; it implies doubtfulness and unsettled waver-
ing of mind.    It is impossible that the course of life can be
any other than uneven and incomposed, if the spring of it,
the heart, whence are the issues of life, be so.    A man that is
not agreed within is like the waves of the sea, of himself ever
fluctuating to and fro, according to the natural instability of
that element, and at the same time exposed to the tossings of
all the waves that arise.

### *Worldly Possessions*

Possessions and all things worldly abide not in one estate,
but are in a more uncertain and irregular inconstancy than
either the flowers and plants of the field, or the moon, from
which they are called sublunary :    like Nebuchadnezzar's
image, degenerating by degrees into baser metals, and in
the end, into a mixture of iron and clay.

### *Sin*

As in religion, so in the course and practice of men's lives
the stream of sin runs from one age into another, and every
age makes it greater, adding somewhat to what it receives,
as rivers grow in their course by the accession of brooks that
fall into them ;    and every man when he is born, falls like a
drop into the main current of corruption, and so is carried
down with it, and this by reason of its strength and his own
nature, which willingly dissolves unto it and runs along
with it.

### *Libera nos Domine*

Deliver me, O Lord, from the errors of wise men, yea, and
of good men.

### All is Grass

There is indeed a great deal of seeming difference betwixt the outward conditions of life amongst men. Shall the rich and honourable and beautiful and healthful go in together, under the same name, with the baser and unhappier part, the poor, wretched sort of the world, who seem to be born for nothing but sufferings and miseries ? At least, hath the wise no advantage beyond the fools ? Is all grass ? Make you no distinction ? No ; *all is grass*, or, if you will have some other name, be it so, once this is true, that all flesh is grass ; and if that glory which shines so much in your eyes must have a difference, then this is all it can have—it is but *the flower* of that same grass ; somewhat above the common grass in gayness, a little comelier, and better apparelled than it, but partaker of its frail and fading nature ; it hath no privilege nor immunity that way ; yea, of the two, it is the less durable, and usually shorter lived ; at the best it decays with it : The grass withereth, and the flower thereof falleth away.

### LAMENT

Happy the craw
That biggs [1] in the Trotten shaw,[2]
And drinks o' the water o' Dye—
For nae mair may I.

[1] Builds.          [2] Wood.

### THE BROOMFIELD HILL

*It seems that a Knight, owing to some subtle spell, fell asleep while waiting for his love in the golden broom, and neither his faithful steed nor his gay goss-hawk could rouse him.   Meanwhile the lady came—strewed roses on the ground as a token that she had been there—and, pitiless, fled away " as licht as a glint o' the moon," never to reappear again.   Perhaps she was of fairy origin.   So, all too late, the unfortunate sleeper awoke to find her gone " far away from heart and eye, and forever far away."*

" O where were ye, my milk-white steed,
    That I hae coft [1] sae dear,
That wadna' watch and waken me
    When there was maiden here ? "

" *I stampèd wi' my foot, master,*
    *And gard my bridle ring,*
*But no kin thing wald waken ye,*
    *Till she was passed and gane.*"

" And wae betide ye, my gas goss-hawk,
    That I did love sae dear,
That wadna' watch and waken me
    When there was maiden here."

" *I clappèd wi' my wings, master,*
    *And aye my bells I rang,*
*And aye cryed, Waken, waken, master,*
    *Before the ladye gang.*"

[1] Bought.

159

"But haste and haste, my guide white steed,
  To come the maiden till,
Or a' the birds of gude green wood
  Of your flesh shall have their fill."

"*Ye need no burst your gude white steed*
  *Wi' racing o'er the howm* [1]*;*
*Nae bird flies faster through the wood,*
  *Than she flew through the broom.*"

## ROBIN REDBREAST'S TESTAMENT

"Gude day, now, bonnie Robin,
  How lang hae ye been here?"
"I've been a bird about this bush
  This mair than twenty year.

"But now I am the sickest bird
  That ever sat on brier ;
And I wad mak' my testament,
  Gudeman, if ye wad hear.

"Gar tak' this bonnie neb o' mine,
  That picks upon the corn ;
And gie't to the Duke o' Hamilton,
  To be a hunting horn.

"Gar tak' thae bonnie feathers o' mine,
  The feathers o' my neb ;
And gie to the Lady Hamilton
  To fill a feather bed.

[1] Green margin of a river.

" Gar tak' this gude richt leg of mine,
 And mend the brig o' Tay ;
It will be a post and pillar gude,
 It will neither bow nor sway.

" And tak' this other leg of mine,
 And mend the brig o' Weir ;
It will be a post and pillar gude,
 It will neither bow nor steer.

" Gar tak' thae bonnie feathers o' mine,
 The feathers o' my tail ;
And gie to the lads o' Hamilton
 To be a barn-flail.

" And tak' thae bonnie feathers o' mine,
 The feathers o' my breast ;
And gie them to the bonnie lad
 Will bring to me a priest."

Now in there cam' my Lady Wren,
 Wi' mony a sigh and groan ;
" O what care I for a' the lads,
 If my ain lad be gone ! "

Then Robin turn'd him round about,
 E'en like a little king ;
" Gae pack ye out at my chamber door,
 Ye little cutty-quean."

*Anon. (circa* 1630).

## COST OF THE BURNING OF TWO MALE WITCHES (KIRKCALDY, 1636)

|  |  |  |  |  |
|---|---|---|---|---|
| *Imprimis.* For ten loads of coal to burn them, five merks........ | £3 | 6 | 8 |
| *Item.* For a tar barrel, 14f...... | 0 | 14 | 0 |
| *Item.* For towes............. | 0 | 6 | 0 |
| *Item.* To him that brought the executioner.................. | 2 | 18 | 0 |
| *Item.* To the excutioner for his pains...................... | 8 | 14 | 0 |
| *Item.* For his expenses here..... | 0 | 16 | 4 |
| *Item.* For one to go to Finmouth for the laird................. | 0 | 6 | 0 |
| Summa town part[1] (Scots) .... | £17 | 1 | 0 |

## FROM THE REPLY OF THE MARQUIS OF HUNTLEY, APRIL 20TH, 1639

*George Gordon, second Marquis of Huntley, one of the few nobles in Scotland who adhered to the King from the very beginning of the troubles, was beheaded in 1649. This was his reply to " certain Noblemen, Gentlemen, and Covenanters of Scotland when they bade him to assist their designs, or be carried to prison."*

Whereas you offer me liberty, I am not so bad a merchant, as to buy it with the loss of my conscience, fidelity, and honour. I have already given my faith to my Prince, upon whose head this crown, by all laws of nature and nations, is justly fallen. I am in your power, and resolved not to leave

---

[1] The " kirk's part " of the expenses runs up to £17 10s., making a grand total of £34 11s., " or (sterling) £2 17s. 7d."

that foul title of traitor as an inheritance upon my posterity.
You may take my head from my shoulders, but not my heart
from my Sovereign.

*Harl. Miscellany, Vol. V.*

## THE TWA CORBIES

*This sinister poem is thought to have been written shortly
after a certain nobleman was treacherously murdered by his
wife in order that she might marry a former lover.*

As I was walking all alane,
I heard twa corbies making a mane,
The tane unto the t'other say,
" Where sall we gang and dine to-day ? "
" In behint[1] yon auld fail dyke,[2]
I wot there lies a new slain knight ;
And nae body kens that he lies there,
But his hawk, his hound, and lady fair.

" His hound is to the hunting gane,
His hawk to fetch the wild-fowl hame,
His lady's ta'en another mate,
So we may mak' our dinner sweet.

" Ye'll sit on his white hause bane,[3]
And I'll pike out his bonny blue een :
Wi' ae lock o' his gowden hair,
We'll theek[4] our nest when it grows bare.

" Mony a one for him makes mane,
But nane sall ken whare he is gane :
O'er his white banes, when they are bare,
The wind sall blaw for evermair."

[1] " Behint," behind.      [2] " Fail dyke," turf wall.
[3] " Hause bane," neck-bone.      [4] " Theek," thatch.

    M 2

## KINDLY KISSES

Kiss'd yestreen, and kiss'd yestreen,
Up the Gallowgate,[1] down the Green :
I've woo'd wi' lords, and woo'd wi' lairds,
I've mool'd [2] wi' carles and mell'd [3] wi' cairds,
I've kiss'd wi' priests—'twas done i' the dark,
Twice in my gown and thrice in my sark ;
But priest, nor lord, nor loon can gie
Sic kindly kisses as he gae me.

## LETTER FROM JAMES HOWELL TO LORD CLIFFORD, EDINBURGH, 1639

MY LORD,

I have seen now all the King of Great Britain's dominions ; and he is a good traveller that hath seen all his dominions. I was born in Wales, I have been in all the four corners of England : I have traversed the diameter of France more than once, and now I am come through Ireland into this kingdom of Scotland. This town of Edinburgh is one of the fairest streets that ever I saw (excepting that of Palermo in Sicily), it is about a mile long, coming sloping down from the castle (called of old the Castle of Virgins, and by Pliny,[4] Castrum Alatum) to Holyroodhouse, now the royal palace ; and these two begin and terminate the town. I am come hither in a very convenient time, for here is a national assembly, and a parliament, my Lord Traquair being his Majesty's Commissioner. The bishops are all gone to wreck and they have had but a sorry funeral ; the very name

[1] Favourite promenade of Glasgow lads and lasses.
[2] Played.            [3] Meddled.
[4] He meant Ptolemy

164

is grown so contemptible that a black dog if he hath any white marks about him, is called Bishop.  Our Lord of Canterbury[1] is grown here so odious, that they call him commonly in the pulpit, the Priest of Baal, and the son of Belial.

I will tell your Lordship of a passage which happened lately in my lodging, which is a tavern.  I had sent for a shoemaker to make me a pair of boots, and my landlord, who is a pert smart man, brought up a chopin of white wine; and for this particular, there are better French wines here than in England and cheaper, for they are but a groat a quart, and it is a crime of a high nature to mingle or sophisticate any wine here.  Over this chopin of white wine, my vintner and shoemaker fell into a hot dispute about bishops.  The shoemaker grew very furious, and called them the firebrands of hell, the panders of the whore of Babylon, and the instruments of the devil ; and that they were of his institution, not of God's.  My vintner took him up smartly and said, " Hold neighbour there, do you not know as well as I, that Titus and Timothy were Bishops ? that our Savour is entitled the Bishop of our Souls ?  That the word Bishop is as frequently mentioned in Scripture as the name Pastor, Elder, or Deacon ?  Then, why do you inveigh so bitterly against them ? "  The shoemaker answered, " I know the name and office to be good, but they have abused it."  My vintner replies, " Well then, you are a shoemaker by your profession, imagine that you, or a hundred, or a thousand, or a hundred thousand of your trade should play the knaves, and sell calf-skin leather boots for neats-leather, or do other cheats, must we therefore go barefoot ?  Must the gentle craft of shoemakers fall therefore to the ground ?  It is the

[1] Archbishop Laud.

165

fault of the men not of the calling." The shoemaker was so gravelled at this, that he was put to his last ; for he had not a word more to say, so my vintner got the day.

There is a fair parliament house built here lately,[1] and it was hoped that his Majesty would have taken the maiden head of it, and come hither to sit in person ; and they did ill who advised him otherwise.

I am to go hence shortly back to Dublin, and so to London, where I hope to find your Lordship, that according to my accustomed boldness I may attend you. In the interim I rest

Your Lordship's most humble servant,

J. H.

### UPON THE DEATH OF CHARLES I.

*James Graham, Marquis of Montrose* (1612–1650), *the brilliant Royalist soldier, " at once his country's glory and her shame," devoted himself to the cause of Charles I. In 1650 he invaded Scotland on behalf of the Stuarts, but was defeated, and captured, and put to death at Edinburgh. The following declaration which he addressed to those who brought him word of his sentence expressed his passionate loyalty :*

*" I am much beholden to the Parliament for the great honour they have decreed me. I am prouder to have my head fixed upon the top of the prison, in the view of the present and succeeding ages, than if they had decreed me a golden statue in the market place, or that my picture should be hung in the king's bedchamber. Would that I had flesh enough to send a portion to every city in Christendom, as a testimony of my unshaken love and fidelity to My King and Country." This speech came*

---

[1] The Parliament House had been built in 1632.

back into the memory of all admirers of Montrose in 1925, when in an auction room in London there were offered for sale to the highest bidder his right arm and hand, and his sword. These relics, well authenticated by accompanying documents, were later withdrawn.

> Great God ! and Just ! could I but rate
> My griefs, and Thy too rigid fate,
> I'd weep the world to such a strain,
> As it should deluge once againe.
> But since thy loud-tongued blood demands supplies,
> More from Briareus' Hands, then Argus' eyes,
> I'll sing thy Obsequies, with trumpet sounds
> And write thy Epitaph with Blood and wounds.

## SOVEREIGNTY IN DANGER

> Can little beasts with lions roar,
> And little birds with eagles soar ?
>
> Can shallow streams command the seas,
> And little ants the humming bees ?
>
> No, no, no, no, it is not meet
> The head should stoop unto the feet.

*Idem.*

## FIDELITY

As truth does not seek corners, it needeth no favour. . . . My resolution is to carry along fidelity and honour to the grave.

*From Montrose's speech to the Scottish Parliament, 1641.*

167

PRIVATE LETTER OF ADVICE WRITTEN BY THE
MARQUIS OF MONTROSE TO CHARLES I. (1641)

SIR,

Your antient and native kingdom of Scotland is in a
mighty distemper. It is incumbent to your Majesty to find
out the disease, remove the causes, and apply convenient
remedies. The disease, in my opinion, is contagious, and
may infect the rest of your Majesty's dominions. It is the
falling sickness ; for they are like to fall from you, and from
the obedience due to you, if, by removing the cause, and
application of wholesome remedies, it be not speedily
prevented. That they intend the overthrow of monarchial
government is a calumny. They are capable of no other,
for many and great reasons ; and ere they will admit another
than your Majesty, and, after you, your son, and nearest of
your posterity, to sit upon that throne, many thousands of
them will spend their dearest blood. You are not like a tree
lately planted, which oweth the fall to the first wind. Your
ancestors have governed there, without interruption of race,
two thousand years, or thereabout, and taken such root as it
can never be plucked up by any but yourselves. If any
other shall entertain such treasonable thoughts, which I do
not believe, certainly they will prove as vain as they are
wicked. The remedy of this dangerous disease consisteth
only in your Majesty's presence for a space in that kingdom.
It is easy to you in person to settle these troubles, and to
disperse these mists of apprehension and mistaking,—impossible to any other. Suffer them not to meddle or dispute
of your power. It is an instrument never subjects yet
handled well. On the other side, aim not at absoluteness :
It endangers your estate, and stirs up troubles : The people

168

of the western parts of the world could never endure it any long time, and they of Scotland less than any. Hearken not to Rehoboam's counsellors : They are flatterers, and therefore cannot be friends : They follow your fortune, and love not your person.

Practice, Sir, the temperate government. It fitteth the humour and disposition of the nation best. It is most strong, most powerful, and most durable of any. It gladdeth the heart of your subjects, and then they erect a throne there for you to reign : *Firmissimum imperium quo obedientes gaudent.* So shall your Majesty secure your authority for the present, and settle it for the future time : Your journey shall be prosperous, your return glorious : You shall be followed with the blessings of your people, and with that contentment which a virtuous deed reflecteth upon the mind of the doer : And more true and solid shall your glory be than if you had conquered nations, and subdued a people.

> " . . . *Pax una, Triumphis*
> *Innumeris potior.*"

*From " Montrose Redivivus," London* (1654).

### ARISE

*This warning was ordered to be read in all the pulpits throughout the kingdom in* 1645, *after divine service, to rouse the Covenanters.*

When we look back upon the great things which God hath done for us, and our former deliverances out of dangers and difficulties, which to us appeared insurmountable, experience breeds hope, and when we consider, how in the midst of all our sorrows and troubles, the Lord our God hath lightened our eyes with the desirable and beautiful sight of his own glory in his temple, we take it for an argument, that he hath yet thoughts of peace, and a purpose of mercy towards us. Though for a small moment he hath forsaken us, yet with great mercies he will gather us. He hath lifted up our enemies, that their fall may be the greater, and that he may cast them down into desolation for ever. Arise! and let us be doing, the Lord of Hosts is with us, the God of Jacob is our refuge.

*Printed Acts of Assembly*, 1645.

RELATION FROM EDINBURGH CONCERNING THE HANGING OF MONTROSE, MAY 21ST, 1650

What with the early going away of the post, and what with the hubbub we are in,—*Montrose being now on the scaffold,*—I must cut short :—

Saturday, he was brought into the town, sitting tied with a rope upon a high chair, upon a cart ; the hangman having before taken off his hat, and riding before him with his bonnet on. Several have been with him. He saith, for personal offences he hath deserved all this ; but justifies his cause. He caused a new suit to be made for himself ; and came yesterday into the Parliament House with a scarlet rochet, and suit of pure cloth all laid with rich lace, a beaver and rich hat-band, and scarlet silk stockings. The Chancellor made a large speech to him, discovering how much formerly he was for the Covenant, and how he hath since broke it. He desired to know whether he might be free to answer ? And being admitted, he told them his cause was good ; and that he had not only a commission, but particular orders for what he had done, from his Majesty, which he was engaged to be a servant to : And he further told them, that, if they would take away his life, the world knew he regarded it not ; that it was a debt that must once be paid ; and that he was willing, and did much rejoice, that he must go the same way his master did ; and it was the joy of his heart, not only to do, but to suffer for him.

His sentence was, to be hanged upon a gallows thirty feet high, three hours, at Edinburgh Cross ; to have his head strucken off, and hanged upon Edinburgh Tolbooth, and his arms and legs to be hanged up in other public towns in the Kingdom, as Glasgow, etc., and his body to be buried at the common burying place, in case excommunication from the Kirk was taken off ; or else to be buried where those are buried that were hanged. All the time, while the sentence was given, and also when he was executed, he seemed no way to be altered, or his spirit moved ; but his speech was full of composure, and his carriage as sweet as ever I saw a man in all my days. When they bid him kneel, he told them he would ; It is absolutely believed that he hath overcome more men by his death, in Scotland, than he would have done if he had lived. For I never saw a more sweeter carriage in a man in all my life. I should write more largely if I had time ; *but he is just now a turning off from the ladder :* but his countenance changes not. But the rest, that came in with him a Saturday, are in great fears. The fatal day being come, designed to put a period to all his troubles, there was erected in the middle of the market place, 'twixt the Cross and Trone, a large four-square scaffold, breast high, in the midst of which was planted a gibbet of thirty feet height. He was convoyed by the Bailies out of the jail, clothed in a scarlet cloak richly shammaded with golden lace. He stept along the streets with so great state, and there appeared in his countenance so much beauty, majesty, and gravity, as amazed the beholders : And many of his enemies did acknowledge him to be the bravest subject in the world ; and in him a gallantry that graced all the croud,—more beseeming a monarch than a mere peer. And in this posture he stept up to the scaffold ; where all his friends and well-wishers being debarred from coming near, they caused a young boy to sit upon the scaffold by him, designed for that purpose, who wrote his last speech in brachography. . . .

When he had done, he called for the executioner, and gave him four pieces of gold ; who, weeping, took his book and declaration, and other printed papers which he had published in his life, and being all tied in a string, hanged them together about his neck, when he said :—" I love this more than my badge of being Knight of the Garter, which his Sacred Majesty was pleased to make me : Nay, more my honour than a chain of gold." And so, with an undaunted courage and gravity, in spite of all their affronts, uncivil and barbarous usage, he went up to the top of that prodigious gibbet.

*From a volume of original manuscripts in the British Museum.*

FROM ''A RELATION OF THE TRUE FUNERAL OF THE GREAT LORD MARQUIS OF MON-TROSE, PRINTED IN THE YEAR 1661."

As the good town of Edinburgh was never wanting to the celebration of loyal solemnities, so they appeared highly magnificent in this ; for their trained bands, in gallant order, ranged both sides of the streets betwixt the two churches ; and, as the corpse of the great Montrose was a laying in the grave of his grandfather, who was viceroy,[1] they did nothing but fire excellent volleys of shot, which were answered with thundering of cannon from the castle : the same was done to the Baron of Delgity, as he was interring by his General's side. There were two things remarkable : the one, that before the beginning of the solemnity, there was nothing but stormy rains ; but the corpse was no sooner come out, but fair weather, with the countenance of the sun, appeared, and continued till all was finished ; and then the clouds returned to their frowns, and the storm began a-fresh. The other, it was observed, that the friends of both the deceased had wedding-countenances ; and their enemies were howling in dark corners, like owls. Some say, that there was then a kind of collective body, or sort of spiritual judicatory in town, that would not be present at the funeral, lest the bones of both should bleed.

*Harl. Miscellany, Vol. VII.*

### ELEGY ON THE MARQUIS OF MONTROSE

In vain thou look'st that I should show
Whose ashes here doth sleep below :
For, if thou wouldst acquainted be
With his great parts and virtues high,
Consult with after-times ; they'll tell
What we delight not to reveal.
Our offspring will the truth discover,
Where we took pains the truth to smother.
Advise with times-recorder : come,
He'll give you reasons why we're dumb ;

[1] The third Earl of Montrose was Chancellor and Viceroy of Scotland in 1505.

My prince bids me but only say,
Montrose's bones we here did lay ;
The pious dust forbids me breath
Aught of his usage or his death,
Lest sober infidels should spy
Our church's weakness, and deny
The Gospel for our sakes, and cry,
" His death's his country's obloquy."

*Anon.*

## REPLY FROM GEORGE OGILVY TO LORD CALLENDAR (1561)

*In this letter George Ogilvy of Barras declines to surrender to Lord Callendar the Scottish Regalia[1]—Crown, Sceptre and Sword of State—which were being preserved from Cromwell, in Dunnottar Castle. They had been brought there on June 6th, 1651—three months before the Battle of Dunbar—at great personal risk by Mrs. Drummond, a minister's wife, who, disguised as a peasant woman, travelled eighty miles " on horseback ryding always near to the sea along the top of high crags," resolving to lose her life rather than give them up. They were preserved in this amazing stronghold, perched high above the fierce coast of Kincardineshire, by a half-starved garrison through a long and desperate siege. When the Estates wished*

---

[1] The Scottish Regalia are very ancient. Edward I., after his defeat of John Baliol in 1296, carried off the Crown of Scotland, and Robert Bruce was forced to have a new one. This, in turn, fell into Edward's rapacious hands ; and because the Countess of Buchan had dared to place it on Bruce's head, she was most carefully confined in a cage built upon one of the towers of Berwick Castle. Another Crown seems to have been made in 1315, after Bannockburn. The present Crown is thought to consist largely of the material of the old one. It has, however, some French work about it which probably dates from the reign of James V.

*to remove them to a place of greater security, Ogilvy replied with stubborn loyalty " neither know I wher they shall be so secure as within the house of Dunotter."*

Sy<sup>r</sup>,

I have receaved yours, wherin I perceive you demand y<sup>e</sup> honours of the Croune intrusted by y<sup>e</sup> Kings [1] Matie to be kept in the house of Dunotter, which demand I may not nor cannot obey without ane order under y<sup>e</sup> Kings Maties hand, neither know I wher they shall be so secure as w<sup>t</sup>in the house of Dunotter. The conditione whereof is in pretie good case for the present, and I hope shall be in better er long, when the meill [2] of the Shyr of Abd. appoynted to be sent heir by y<sup>e</sup> Comitie of Estait, comes heir, whilk I humbly intreat you will cause hasten, since y<sup>e</sup> enemy (as I am crediblie informed) is retired towards Dundie. The Comitie for the shyr did not keip the last meiting by reasone of ane suden alarme from y<sup>e</sup> enemie, bot I shall stryve to have a meiting with all conveniencie whereby I shall know ther resolution. Collonell George Keith hath sent no servand heir, neither have I heard of any that is come frome him. Expecting assystance frome your lo/ in case of necessitie to him, who in all his actions shall approve himselff to be

For

The rytt Hono<sup>ll</sup>

his most assurit louing

freind

GEORG OGILVIE of

BARRAS.

[1] Charles II. had been crowned at Scone on January 1st, 1651.
[2] Meal which never reached the garrison.

## HALLO! MY FANCY

*The first six stanzas of this fantastic poem were anonymous, and well known in the beginning of the seventeenth century. The other verses were added later, " being writ by Lieutenant William Cleland (1661–1689) in the College of Edinburgh, and 18 years of Age." He was later the heroic defender of Dunkeld.*

In melancholic fancy,
        Out of myself,
In the vulcan dancy,
All the world surveying,
Nowhere staying,
    Just like a fairy elf ;
Out o'er the tops of highest mountains skipping,
Out o'er the hill, the trees and valleys tripping,
Out o'er the ocean seas, without an oar or shipping,—
    *Hallo ! my fancy, whither wilt thou go ?*


Amidst the misty vapours
Fain would I know
What doth cause the tapers ;
Why the clouds benight us
And affright us.
    While we travel here below ;
Fain would I know what makes the roaring thunder,
And what these lightnings be that rend the clouds asunder,
And what these comets are on which we gaze and wonder—
    *Hallo ! my fancy, whither wilt thou go ?*

Fain would I know the reason,
Why the little ant,
All the summer season,
Layeth up provision
On condition
To know no winter's want.
And how housewives, that are so good and painful,
Do unto their husbands prove so good and gainful ;
And why the lazy drones to them do prove disdainful—
*Hallo ! my fancy, whither wilt thou go?* . . .

When I look before me,
There I do behold
There's none that sees or knows me ;
All the world's a-gadding,
Running madding ;
None doth his station hold.
He that is below envieth him that riseth,
And he that is above, him that's below despiseth,
So every man his plot and counter-plot deviseth.
*Hallo ! my fancy, whither wilt thou go?*

Amidst the foamy ocean,
Fain would I know
What doth cause the motion,
And returning
In its journeying,
And doth so seldom swerve ?
And how the little fishes that swim beneath salt waters,
Do never blind their eye ; methinks it is a matter
An inch above the reach of old Erra Pater !—
*Hallo ! my fancy, whither wilt thou go?*

Fain would I be resolved
How things are done ;
And where the bull¹ was calved
Of bloody Phalaris,
And where the tailor is
That works to the man i' the moon !
Fain would I know how Cupid aims so rightly ;
And how the little fairies do dance and leap so lightly,
And where fair Cynthia makes her ambles nightly—
*Hallo ! my fancy, whither wilt thou go ?*

*In Conceit, like Phaeton,*
*I'll mount Phœbus' Chair !*
*Having ne'er a Hat on,*
*All my Hair's a-burning,*
*In my journeying,*
*Hurrying through the Air.*
*Fain would I hear his fiery Horses neighing !*
*And see how they on foamy Bitts are playing !*
*All the Stars and Planets I will be surveying !*
*Hallo ! my fancy, whither wilt thou go ?*

*O from what ground of Nature,*
*Doth the Pelican,*
*That self-devouring Creature*
*Prove so froward,*
*And untoward,*
*Her Vitals for to strain !*
*And why the subtile Fox, while in Death's wounds is lying !*
*Doth not lament his Pangs by howling and by crying !*
*And why the milk-white Swan doth sing when she is dying !*
*Hallo ! my fancy, whither wilt thou go ?*

¹ This bull was of brass.

178

*Fain would I conclude this,*
*At least make Essay,*
*What similitude is,*
*Why Fowls of a Feather,*
*Flock and fly together,*
*And lambs know Beasts of Prey!*
*Now Nature's Alchymists, these small laborious Creatures,*
*Acknowledge still a Prince in ordering their Matters*
*And suffer none to live, who slothing, lose their Features!*
*Hallo! my fancy, whither wilt thou go?*

*Fain also would I prove this,*
*By considering,*
*What that, which you call Love, is :*
*Whether it be Folly,*
*Or a melancholy,*
*Or some Heroick thing!*
*Fain I'd have it prov'd, by one whom Love hath wounded,*
*And fully upon one his Desire hath founded,*
*Whom nothing else could please, tho' the World were rounded!*
*Hallo! my fancy, whither wilt thou go?*

*Hallo! my fancy, hallo!*
*Stay, stay at home with me,*
*I can thee no longer follow ;*
*For thou hast betrayed me,*
*And bewray'd me ;*
*It is too much for thee.*
*Stay, stay at Home with me, leave off thy lofty Soaring,*
*Stay thou at Home with me and on thy Books be poring.*
*For he that goes abroad, lays little up in Storing.*
*Thou'rt welcome Home, my Fancy, welcome home to me.*

## THE COAT OF ARMS OF SIR JOHN PRESBYTER

*This is a time-serving skit upon the Presbyterian faction. " Sir John " was a clerical appellation, used originally in a respectful sense, but which afterwards became appropriated by the " canting crew," to scurrility and abuse. Presbyter is, of course, derived from the Greek πρεσβύτερος = an elder.*

He bears, Party per Pale indented, God's glory, and his own interest ; over all, honour, profit, pleasure counter-changed ; ensigned with a helmet of Ignorance, opened with Confidence befitting his degree, mantled with Gules and Tyranny, doubled with Hypocrisy over a wreath of Pride and Covetousness : for his crest, a sinister hand, holding up a solemn league and covenant, reversed and torn : in a scroll, underneath the shield, these words for his motto, *Aut hoc, aut nihil.*

This coat-armour is dupalled with another of four pieces, signifying thereby his four matches.

The first is of the family of Amsterdam : she bears for her arms, in a field of Toleration, three Jews' heads proper, with as many blue caps on them.

The second is of the house of Geneva : she bears for her arms, in a field of Separation, marginal notes on the Bible false quoted.

The third is of the country of New England : she bears, for her arms, a prick-eared Preachman, perched upon a pulpit proper, holding forth to the people a schismatical directory.

The fourth and last is Scotland : she bears in escutcheon the field of Rebellion, charged with a stool of repentance.

*Printed in the year* 1658. *Harleian Miscellany, Vol. X.*

## GOD HATH LAID ENGAGEMENTS UPON SCOTLAND

*Archibald Campbell, Marquis of Argyll* (1598–1661), *strongly opposed the execution of Charles I., and in 1651 crowned Charles II. at Scone. After the defeat of Worcester, he defended himself for nearly a year in his Castle of Inverary against Cromwell's troops ; but in 1652 gave in his submission to the Protector. On the Restoration he repaired to Whitehall, but was committed to the Tower, and later taken to Edinburgh, and after a mock trial beheaded.*

God hath laid engagements upon Scotland. We are tyed by covenant to religion and reformation ; those that were then unborn are engaged to it, and in our baptism we are engaged to it, and it passes the power of any under Heaven to absolve a man from the oath of God. Those that are the best subjects are the best Christians. And that I am looked on as a friend to reformation is my glory. These times are like to be very sinning times or very suffering times. Let Christians take their choice. There is a sad dilemma in the business : sin or suffer . . . Truly he that will chose the better part will chose to suffer. Others that will chose to sin shall not escape suffering. They shall suffer too. . . . Not as I do here, but worse. Mine is but temporal. Theirs shall be eternal. When I shall be singing, they shall be howling. Beware therefore of sin in such times. I desire not that the Lord should judge any man. Nor do I judge any but myself. I wish that as the Lord may pardon me, so may he pardon them for this and other things, and that what they have done to me may never meet them in their accounts. I have no more to say, but to beg the

Lord, that since I go away, he may bless them that stay behind.

*From the Speech of the Marquis of Argyll, made on the Scaffold, May 27th, 1661. Harleian Miscellany, Vol. IX. (Sup. I.).*

## "THOU SHALT NOT SUFFER A WITCH TO LIVE"

*Isobel Gowdie, who was burned as a witch [1] in 1662, tells us in her Confessions that she always used the following charm when she wished to change herself into a hare.*

> " I sall go intill a hare,
> With sorrow, sigh, and muckle care ;
> And I sall go in the devil's name,
> Ay while I come back again."

The devil would send me now and then to Aulderne on some errands to my neighbours, in the shape of a hare. I was one morning, about the break of the day, going to Aulderne in the shape of a hare, and Patrick Papley's servants, in Kilhill, being going to their labouring, his hounds being with them, ran after me, being in the shape of a hare. I ran very long, but was forced, being weary, at last to take to my own house. The door being left open, I ran in behind a chest, and the hounds followed in ; but they went to the other side of the chest, and I was forced to run forth again, and ran into another house, and there took leisure to say—

> " Hare, hare, God send thee care ;
> I am in a hare's likeness now,
> But I sall be a woman e'en now ;
> Hare, hare, God send thee care,"

---

[1] Whoever would understand how completely even the most enlightened minds of that age were under the dominion of superstition should turn to Henry More's " Antidote against Atheism."

and so I returned to my own shape, as I am at this instant, again. The dogs will sometimes get some bites of us when we are in hares, but will not get us killed. When we turn out of a hare's likeness to our own shape we will have the bites and rives and scratches on our bodies. When we would be in the shape of cats we did nothing but cry and wraw, and riving, and, as it were, worrying one another! and when we come to our shapes again we will find the scratches and rives on our skin very sore. When one of us, or more, are in the shape of cats, and meet with any others, our neighbours, we will say—

> " Devil speed thee,
> Go thou with me ! "

and immediately they will turn in the shape of a cat and go with us. When we will be in the shape of crows we will be larger than ordinary crows, and will sit upon branches of trees.

*From " Criminal Trials in Scotland, 1484–1624,"*
*edited by Robert Pitcairn.*


### EPITAPH

*At Hamilton lie the heads of John Parker, James Hamilton, and Christopher Strang, who suffered at Edinburgh 7th December, 1666.*

> Stay passenger, take notice
> What thou reads
> At Edinboro be our bodies
> Here our heads ;
> Our right hands stood at Lanark
> These we want
> Because with them we sware
> The Covenant.

183

## EPITAPH ON ANNA GORDON

Hier lyes inclosed within this little shrine
The precious body of a soul divine.
The souls returned to God who did it give
To sing His praise, and shal forever live.
The body, which with beautie was adorned,
Must now to dust from whence it was returned.
But yet in remembrance of hir virtue shal
Indure from age to age perpetual.
As Pallas she hir wisdom still did show ;
As Pytho she in eloquence did flow ;
And Juno, who in riches did excel,
Was not more free nor yet more hospital.
The poor she fed, the naked clad also ;
None hungry, naked from hir house did go.
Of beautie, manners, and humility
A perfect patterns he . . .
. . . And these her life did grace
And showed her descent of a worthy race.
So hier the Pheynix of hir tyme doth ly,
Who lived unspotedly and blest did dy.    1672.

## THE YULE DAYS

*Yule or Iol, the great annual festival of the ancient Scandi-
navians in honour of Freya, son of Odin, was a time of unlimited
feasting and dancing, and upon it the early Christians ingrafted
the festival of the Nativity, in order to disturb as little as
possible the traditions of the people.  The word seems to have
been derived from the Celtic " Hiaul," which signifies sun.
Everywhere among the Celts a solemn feast was celebrated
during the winter solstice as a welcome to the sun when it*

*returned once more to the heavens. The sun-log or Yule log, because it was round in shape, was, at a very remote period, cherished as the symbol of the great solar luminary. Thus we still have a trace of the original Sun-worship in our midst.*

The king sent his lady on the first Yule day,
A papingo-aye ; [1]
*Wha learns my carol and carries it away?*

The king sent his lady on the second Yule day,
Three partridges, a papingo-aye ;
*Wha learns my carol and carries it away?*

The king sent his lady on the third Yule day,
Three plovers, three partridges, a papingo-aye ;
*Wha learns my carol and carries it away?*

The king sent his lady on the fourth Yule day,
A goose that was gray,
Three plovers, three partridges, a papingo-aye ;
*Wha learns my carol and carries it away?*

The king sent his lady on the fifth Yule day,
Three starlings, a goose that was gray,
Three plovers, three partridges, and a papingo-aye ;
*Wha learns my carol and carries it away?*

The king sent his lady on the sixth Yule day,
Three goldspinks, three starlings, a goose that was gray,
Three plovers, three partridges, and a papingo-aye ;
*Wha learns my carol and carries it away?*

[1] Peacock.

185

The king sent his lady on the seventh Yule day,
A bull that was brown, three goldspinks, three starlings,
A goose that was gray,
Three plovers, three partridges, and a papingo-aye ;
*Wha learns my carol and carries it away?*

*Anon.*

### TWELFTH DAY

*This is a memory game which used to be played on Twelfth Day or Epiphany, after the bean had been discovered in the Twelfth Cake. It is a relic of the Roman Saturnalia, at the close of which festival the Roman children drew lots with beans to see who would be king.*

What will be our twelve, boys ?
What will be our twelve, boys ?
Twelve's the Twelve Apostles ;
Eleven's maidens in a dance ;
Ten's the Ten Commandments ;
Nine's the Muses o' Parnassus ;
Eight's the table rangers ;
Seven's the stars of heaven ;
Six the echoing waters ;
Five's the hymnlers o' my bower ;
Four's the gospel-makers ;
Three, three thrivers ;
Twa's the lily and the rose,
That shine baith red and green, boys ;
My only ane, she walks alane,
And evermair has dune, boys.

186

FROM ''THE SCOTS GARD'NER, PUBLISHED FOR THE CLIMATE OF SCOTLAND,'' 1683

*Mr. John Reid was gardener to Sir George Mackenzie, of Rosehaugh. He published this practical garden book in the reign of Charles II., just fifty years after John Parkinson's " Paradisi in Sole, Paradisus Terrestris " appeared.*

I

As the sun is the centre of this world ; as the heart of man is the centre of man ; as the nose is the centre of the face ; and as it is unseemly to see a man wanting a leg, one arme, &c.; or his nose standing at one side the face, or not straight ; or wanting a cheek, ane eye, ane ear ; or with one (or all of them) great at one side and small on the other ; just so with house-courts, avenues, gardens, orchards, &c., where regularity or uniformity is not observed.

2

The black cherrie or geen is a tree that I love well in avenues and thickets ; there is a sort at Niddrie-Castle, where I was born, seven miles West from Edinburgh, whose fruit is preferable to any cherrie : I take it for a sort of heart, but it's a great bearer (which propertie the heart-cherrie wants), they are best stocks for standard cherries. The learned Evelyn and the ingenious Cook take notice of this tree.

3

There is no way under the sun so probable for improving our land, as inclosing and planting the same. Therefore I wish it were effectually put in practice.

*John Reid, Gard'ner.*

### CROSSING THE BAR

*The following lines, written by Donald Cargill, Covenanter, shortly before his execution in 1681, to his friend James Skene, contain a metaphor which Tennyson made familiar to the world.*

The God of mercies grant you a full gale and a fair entry into his kingdom, which may carry you sweetly and swiftly over the bar, that you find not the rub of Death.

### FROM A LETTER OF JANET LINTOUN (1685)

*Janet Lintoun, a Covenanting prisoner in Dunnottar Castle, writes in a gallant spirit to her husband from the prison whence she expected to pass only to banishment.*

My dear heart, bless the Lord on my behalf, that ever it should hav pleased such a holy God to have looked upon such an unworthy sinner as I am, or to hav honoured the like of me to suffer anay thing for his name's saik, or bear his cross in a day when ther is so few longing to wear his livery. . . . The Lord has made all things easy to me and he has been soe kind to my soul somtyms since I came to prison, that I counted all things nothing in comparison of him. . . . *Now*, my dear, ye are dear, indeed, to me, bot not soe dear as Christ. . . . My love, I ken not what the Lord will doe with me ; bot I think I will see you although I should be banished out of my nativ land. Although enemies have separat our bodies, they shall never separat my love from you. . . .

### FALSE LUVE

Fals luve ! and hae ye played me this
In the simmer, mid the flowers ?
I sall repay ye back again
In the winter, mid the showers !

Bot again, dear luve, and again, dear luve,
Will ye not turn again ?
As ye look to ither women,
Sall I to ither men.

*Anon.*

### THE MISFORTUNES OF SCOTLAND

*George Lockhart* (1673–1731), *Laird of Carnwath, was a Jacobite M.P. and one of the Commissioners for the Treaty of Union.*

It is beyond the reach of Man to assign Reasons for the good or bad Fate that attends Kingdoms, Families, or single Persons (for the Ways of God are past finding out) ; yet there are two Considerations that I have often reflected on to have had a great share in bringing down those Judgments which have of late fallen upon the Kings and Kingdom of *Scotland* : For since the Union of the two Crowns many and heavy have been the Misfortunes of both. The first is, the mean spirited Behaviour of K[ing] J[ames] VI. in not revenging his Mother's Murder. Ought he, with a View of not irritating Queen *Elizabeth*, been guilty of such an unnatural Submission ? And was it not a servile Acknowledgment of *England*'s Dominion to suffer the sacred Person of the Queen of *Scotland* to be Tried, Condemned, and Executed, without so much as daring to say it was ill done ?

And was it not a Connivance at the greatest Violation and Encroachment that was ever offered to the Divine Rights of crowned Heads, thus silently to see her treated after such a manner, who was accountable to none but God? How much was he degenerated from the illustrious and generous Stock from whence he sprung? And which of his Royal Progenitors would not have resented it with Fire and Sword? For my part, I'm afraid the Indignation of God was stirred up upon this Account against his Posterity, and that particularly in the Case of his Son, *Charles* 1., God visited the Iniquity of his Father, committed by shewing so little Duty and natural Affection to his Mother, and regard and value for the sacred Rights of crowned Heads. For tho' we often read of Conquerors having dispatched conquered Kings, and Subjects murdering their Soveraigns, yet she was the first Instance of a Royal Pannel, and the only Precedent to the hard Fate of her Grandson.

*Memoirs concerning the Affairs of Scotland* (*London*, 1714).

### GILLESPIE'S END

It came to that, he keept his chamber still to his death, wearing and wasting, hoasting [coughing] and sweating. Ten dayes before his death his sweating went away, and his hoasting lesned, yet his weaknes still encreased. His wife seeing the time draw near, spake to him and said, " The time of your releife is nou near and hard at hand ! " He answered, " I long for that time ! O happy they that are there ! " This was the last word he was heard sensibly to speak. Mr. Frederick Carmichael being there, they went to prayer, expecting death so suddenly. In the midst of prayer he left his ratling, and the pangs and fetches of death began ; thence his senses went away. Wherupon they rose from prayer, and beheld till in a very gentle manner the pinns of his tabernacle wer loosed.

*Robert Wodrow* (1679–1734).

## THE MARTYRS' MEMORIAL, GREYFRIARS' CHURCHYARD, EDINBURGH, 1688

*In the southern annexe of Greyfriars' Churchyard, were confined the Covenanting prisoners whom the gaols, already filled to overflowing with the adherents of this cause, could not hold ; and large numbers of them died under the rigours of the winter. Here too the Covenant was signed in 1638 on the " throuchstone " or horizontal gravestone on the south side of the church. By far the most interesting memorial, however, in the churchyard is the one called the Martyrs' Monument, with its pathetic inscription—*

Halt passengers take heed what you do see,
This tomb doth shew for what some men did die.
Here lies interr'd the dust of those who stood
'Gainst perjury, resisting unto blood ;
Adhering to the Covenants and laws
Establishing the fame, which was the cause
Then lives were sacrific'd unto the lust
Of Prelatists abjur'd. Though here their dust
Lies mixt with murderers, and other crew,
Who justice justly did to death pursue ;
But as for them, no cause was to be found
Worthy of death, but only they were found,
Constant and stedfast, zealous, witnessing
For the Prerogatives of CHRIST their KING,

Which truths were seal'd by famous Guthrie's head
And all along to Mr. Renwick's blood
They did endure the wrath of enemies,
Reproaches, torments, deaths and injuries,
But yet they're those who from such troubles came,
And now triumph in glory with the LAMB.

### TWO OLD RHYMES

#### I

Give liberalye to neidful folke,
Denye nane of them al
For little thou knawest heirin this lyf
Quhat chaunce may thee befall.

#### 2

A nice wife and a back doore,
Oft maketh a rich man poore.

### RING POSY

Tho far apairt
Yet neare in hairte.

### FROM "THE SECRET COMMONWEALTH"

*Somnia, terrores magicos, miracula, sagas,*
*Nocturnos lemures portentaque Thessala rides?*

*Hor. 2 Ep.* 11, 208.

Fairies are said to be of a middle nature, betwixt man and
angel, as were demons thought to be of old; of intelligent
studious spirits, and light changeable bodies (lyke those
called astral), somewhat of the nature of a condensed cloud,
and best seen in twilight. Their bodies be so pliable,

through the subtilty of the spirits that agitate them, that they can make them appear or disappear at pleasure. Some have bodies or vehicles so spongious, thin, and defecate, that they are fed by only sucking into some fine spirituous liquors, that pierce lyke pure air and oil : others feed more gross, on the foyson or substance of corns and liquors, or corne itself that grows on the surface of the earth, which these fairies steall away, partly invisible, partly preying on the grain, as do crows and mice ; wherefore, in this same age, they are sometimes heard to bake bread, strike hammers, and to do such like services within the little hillocks they most haunt : some whereof of old, before the Gospell dispell'd paganism, and in some barbarous places as yet, enter houses after all are at rest, and set the kitchens in order, cleansing all the vessels. Such drags go under the name of Brownies.

Of these invisible wights the womenkind are said to Spin very fine, to Dy, to Tossue, and Embroyder, but whether only curious Cob-webs, impalpable Rainbows . . . I leave to conjecture.

*Robert Kirk, Minister at Aberfoill,* 1691.

## THE SECOND SIGHT, 1699

*Samuel Pepys, always a curious enquirer, was anxious for information concerning " the second sight of which people were so persuaded in the Highlands and Isles, that one would be more laught at for not believing it there than affirming it elsewhere." The following letter from Lord Tarbat to Mr. Boyle in* 1699 *was forwarded to him by Lord Reay.*

Sir, I heard very much, but beleived very litle of the *second sight,* yet its being afirmed by severall of great veracitie,

I was enduced to make some enquerie after it in the yeir 1652, being then confyned to abyde in the north of Scoteland by the English usurpers. The more generall accompts of it were, That many Highlanders, yet farr more Islanders, were quallified with this sight ; That men, women, and children indistinctly[1] were subject (to) it, and children where parents were not, and sometyme people come to age who had it not when young ; Nor could any tell me by what meanes produced. It's a trouble to most of them who are subject to it, and they would be rid of it at any rate if they could. The sight is of no long duratione, only continually so long as they keep their eyes steadie, without trembling.

\*     \*     \*     \*     \*

That which generally is seen by them are the species[2] of liveing creatures, and of animat[3] things which are in motione, such as shipps and habites uppone persones. They never sie the species of any persone who is allreadie dead. What they forsie fails not to existe in the mode and in that place where it appears to them. They can not tell what space of tyme shall interveen betwixt the aparitione and reall existance, but some of the hardiest and longest experience have some rules for conjectures : as if they sie a man with a shrowding sheet in the apparitione, they would conjecture at the neirnes and remotenes of his death by the more or less of his bodie that is covered by it. They will ordinarely sie ther absent freinds, though at a great distance, sometymes no less than from America to Scoteland, sitting, standing, or walking in some certaine place ; and then they conclude with assurance that they will sie them so and there.

\*     \*     \*     \*     \*

[1] Indiscriminately.          [2] Images, phantoms.
[3] Perhaps written by mistake for inanimate.

194

I wes once travelling in the Highlands, and a good number of servants with me, as is usuall ther, and one of them goeing a litle befor me, entereing unto a house where I was to stay all night, and goeing hastily to the doore, he suddenly start back with a scrich and did fall by a stone that hitt his foot. I asked what the matter wes, for hee seemed to me to be very much frighted. He told me very seriouslie that I should not lodge in that house, because shortly a dead coffine would be caryed out of it, for many were caryeing it when hee wes herd cry. I neglecting his words and staying there, he said to others of the servents he wes very sorie for it, and that what hee saw would surely come to pass, and though no sick persone wes then there, yet the landlord, a healthie Highlander, dyed of ane applextick fitt befor I left the house.

*   *   *   *   *

Among the accompts given me by Sir Normade McLeod, ther wes one worthie of speciall nottice, which wes this. Ther wes a gentleman in the Isle of Harris who was alwayes seen by the seers with ane arrow in his thigh ; such in the Isle who thought these prognosticationes infallable did not doubt but hee would be shott in the thigh befor hee dyed. Sir Normade told me that hee heard it the subject of there discourse for many years when that gentleman wes present. At last he dyed without any such accident. Sir Normed was at his buriall at St. Clement's Church in the Harris. At the same tyme the corpse of ane other gentleman wes brought to be buried in the same very church. The frends on either syde cam to debeat who should first enter the church, and in a trice from words they came to blowes. One of the number (who wes armed with bow and arrowes)

o 2

let one fly amonge them. (Now every famely in that Isle
have ther burriall place in the church in stone chests, and
the bod(i)es are caryed in oppin beers to the bur(i)all place.)
Sir Normande haveing apeased the tumult, one of the arrowes
wes found shot in the dead man's thigh ; to this Sir Normand
himself wes a witness.

\* \* \* \* \*

But a hint may be taken from this image mentioned by
Aristotle in the 4th of his Metaphysicks, if I remember right,
for it's long since I read it ; as alsoe from that comone
opinione that young infants (unsoyled with many objects)
doe see apparitions which are not seen by those of older
years ; lykeways from this, that severall who did see the
second sight when in the Highlands or Isles, yet when
transported to live in other countreys, especially in America,
they quite lose this qualitie, as wes told me by a gentleman
who knew some of them in Barbados who did sie no visione
ther, although he knew them to be seers when they lived in
the Isles of Scotland.

### THE LAMENT OF THE WEARY GHOST

" *Unhappy ghost, go waile thy griefe below*
*Where never soule but endless horror sees.*"

Wae's me, wae's me,
The acorn's not yet
Fallen from the tree
That's to grow the wood,
That's to make the cradle,
That's to rock the bairn,
That's to grow a man,
That's to lay me.

## AT MOFFAT

We here met with good wine, and some mutton pretty well drest ; but looking into our beds, found there was no lying in them, so we kept on our cloaths all night and enjoyed ourselves by a good fire, making often protestations never to come into that country again.

*From " The Journey to Edenborough,"*
*by Joseph Taylor,* 1705.

## THE BIRKS OF INVERMAY

The smiling morn, the breathing spring,
Invite the tuneful birds to sing ;
And while they warble from each spray,
Love melts the universal lay.
Let us, Amanda, timely wise,
Like them improve the hour that flies,
And in soft raptures waste the day
Among the birks of Invermay.

For soon the winter of the year,
And age, life's winter, will appear ;
At this, thy living bloom will fade,
As that will strip the verdant shade :
Our taste of pleasure then is o'er ;
The feather'd songsters love no more ;
And when they droop, and we decay,
Adieu the birks of Invermay.

*David Malet* (1700-1765).

FROM THE SPEECH ON THE UNION OF SCOTLAND
AND ENGLAND, NOVEMBER 2ND, 1706

*Lord Belhaven was the only peer who opposed the Act of
Succession in Scotland, when the Duke of York was present,
for which he was imprisoned in Edinburgh Castle. He is
described as having been a " rough, fat, black, noisy man ;
more like a butcher than a lord."*

I think I see a free and independent kingdom delivering
up that which all the world hath been fighting for since the
days of Nimrod ; yea, that for which most of all the empires,
kingdoms, states, principalities, and the dukedoms of Europe
are at this time engaged in the most bloody and cruel wars ;
to wit, a power to manage their own affairs by themselves,
without the assistance and counsel of any other. . . .

I think I see the noble and honourable peerage of Scotland,
whose valiant predecessors led armies against their enemies
upon their own proper charges and expense, now divested of
their followers and vassalages ; and put upon such an equal
foot with their vassals, that I think I see a petty English
exciseman receive more homage and respect than what was
paid formerly to their *quondam* MacCallammores. . . .

But above all, my Lord, I think I see our ancient mother,
Caledonia, like Cæsar, sitting in the midst of our senate,
ruefully looking round about her, covering herself with her
royal garment, attending the fatal blow, and breathing out
her last with an *et tu quoque mi fili !* . . .

My Lord Chancellor, the greatest honour that was done
unto a Roman was to allow him the glory of a triumph ; the
greatest and most dishonourable punishment was that of a
parricide. He that was guilty of parricide was beaten with
rods upon his naked body till the blood gushed out of all the

veins of his body ; then he was sewed up in a leathern sack called a *culeus*, with a cock, a viper, and an ape, and thrown headlong into the sea. . . .

My Lord, patricide is a greater crime than parricide, all the world over. . . .

*John Hamilton, Lord Belhaven, at the*
*Scottish Parliament House.*

## HATCHWAY'S EPITAPH ON COMMODORE TRUNNION

*Tobias Smollett* (1721-1771), *called by Austin Dobson the " bourru bienfaisant," was educated at Glasgow, and later took service as a surgeon's mate on one of the vessels of the Carthagena Expedition in* 1741. *He left the Fleet at Jamaica, and after remaining there for several years returned to London, and, failing as a physician, devoted himself to literature.*

Here lies, foundered in a fathom and a half, the shell of Hawser Trunnion, formerly commander of a squadron in his Majesty's service, who broached to at 5 P.M. Oct. x. in the year of his age threescore and nineteen. He kept his guns always loaded, and his tackle ready manned, and never showed his poop to the enemy, except when he took her in tow ; but his shot being expended, his match burnt out, and his upper works decayed, he was sunk by death's superior weight of metal. Nevertheless he will be weighed again at the Great Day, his rigging refitted, and his timbers repaired, and, with one broadside, make his adversary strike in his turn.

*From " Peregrine Pickle."*

## THE VALE OF LEVEN

The water of Leven, though nothing near so considerable as the Clyde, is much more transparent, pastoral, and delightful. This charming stream is the outlet of Loch Lomond, and through a track of four miles pursues its winding course over a bed of pebbles, till it joins the Firth of Clyde at Dumbarton. On this spot stands the castle formerly called Alcluyd, and washed by these two rivers on all sides except a narrow isthmus, which at every spring-tide is overflowed ; the whole is a great curiosity, from the quality and form of the rock, as from the nature of its situation. A very little above the source of the Leven, on the lake, stands the house of Cameron, belonging to Mr. Smollett (the late commissary), so embosomed in oak wood that we did not perceive it till we were within fifty yards of the door. I have seen the Lago di Garda, Albano, di Vico, Bolsena, and Geneva, and I prefer Loch Lomond to them all—a preference which is certainly owing to the verdant islands that seem to float upon its surface, affording the most enchanting objects of repose to the excursive view. Nor are the banks destitute of beauties which can partake of the sublime. On this side they display a sweet variety of wood-land, cornfield, and pasture, with several agreeable villas, emerging, as it were, out of the lake, till at some distance the prospect terminates in huge mountains, covered with heath, which, being in the bloom, affords a very rich covering of purple. Everything here is romantic beyond imagination. This country is justly styled the Arcadia of Scotland ; I do not doubt but it may vie with Arcadia in everything but climate. I am sure it excels it in verdure, wood, and water.

*From " Humphrey Clinker."*

LETTER TO MISS FLORA MACDONALD, FROM
ROBERT FORBES, BISHOP OF ROSS AND CAITH-
NESS, JULY 11TH, 1750

*Flora MacDonald, described by Dr. Johnson as " of middle
stature, soft features, gentle manners and elegant presence,"
was born in 1722 in South Uist. She conducted Prince Charles
Edward, disguised as " Betty Bourke," from Benbecula to
Portree in 1746, and this gallant adventure endeared her to the
heart of every Jacobite.*

MADAM,

The agreeable accounts of your safe arrival at Arma-
dale by your letter to Miss Main, afforded me no small
pleasure, as I will ever think myself interested in every
event of life that happens to Miss Flora MacDonald whether
prosperous or adverse ; a mixture of which we must pass
through in this lower state, which is a chequered scene at
best. You have already experienced both sides of fortune,
and your conduct, in each of them has engaged the attention
of the public, and has justly entitled you to the esteem of
every well thinking person. You have had a recent instance
of that blending of sweet and bitter which inseparably
attends the transactions of human life. Methinks I feel
somewhat of that mixture of joy and grief which would
ensue upon your first meeting with your mother—joy to see
one another once more in health and safety, but grief in
your mutual condolences for the affecting loss of two hopeful
youths ; if we dare take upon ourselves to call anything a loss
that comes from the unerring appointment of Heaven.
May God support you both under the trying affliction and
grant all concerned in it the happy and proper effects of it.
I heartily wish you all things good and happy, and sincerely

am, Madam, your most affectionate friend and very humble servant,

ROBERT FORBES.

### UPON THE DEATH OF ARTHUR, LORD BALMERINO,

*Who left the services of George III., in which he bore some rank, to join the sinking cause of James, after the woeful defeat at Dumblane. He was beheaded upon Tower Hill on August 18th, 1746.*

> Here Arthur lies, the rest forbear ;
> There may be treason in a tear,
> Yet this bold soger may find room
> Where sceptred tyrants dare not come.

### LETTER FROM JAMES BOSWELL TO DAVID GARRICK, INVERNESS, SUNDAY, 29 AUGUST, 1773

MY DEAR SIR,

Here I am, and Mr. Samuel Johnson actually with me. We were a night at Fores, in coming to which, in the dusk of the evening, we passed over the bleak and blasted heath where Macbeth met the witches. Your old preceptor repeated, with much solemnity, the speech—

> " How far is't called to Fores ? What are these,
> So wither'd and so wild in their attire," &c.

This day we visited the ruins of Macbeth's castle at Inverness. I have had great romantick satisfaction in seeing Johnson upon the classical scenes of Shakspeare in Scotland ; which I really looked upon as almost as improbable as that " Birnam wood should come to Dunsinane." Indeed, as I have always been accustomed to view him as a permanent London object, it would not be much more wonderful to me to see St. Paul's church moving along where we now are. As yet we have travelled in post-chaises ; but to-morrow we are to mount on horseback, and ascend into the mountains by Fort Augustus, and so on to the ferry, where we are to cross to Sky. We shall see that Island fully, and then visit some more of the Hebrides ; after which we are to land in Argyleshire, proceed by Glasgow to Auchinleck, repose there a competent time, and then return to Edinburgh, from whence the Rambler will depart for old England again, as soon as he finds it convenient. Hitherto we have had a very prosperous expedition. I flatter myself, *servetur ad imum, qualis ab incepto processerit*. He is in excellent spirits, and I have a rich journnal of his conversation. Look back, *Davy*, to Litchfield ;—run up through the time that has elapsed since you first knew Mr. Johnson,—and enjoy with me his present extraordinary Tour. I could not resist the impulse of writing to you from this place. The situation of the old castle corresponds exactly to Shakspeare's description. While we were there to-day, it happened oddly, that a raven perched upon one of the chimney-tops, and croaked. Then I in my turn repeated—

> " The raven himself is hoarse,
> That croaks the fatal entrance of Duncan,
> Under my battlements."

I wish you had been with us. Think what enthusiastick happiness I shall have to see Mr. Samuel Johnson walking among the romantick rocks and woods of my ancestors at Auchinleck ! Write to me at Edinburgh. You owe me his verses on great George and tuneful Cibber, and the bad

verses which led him to make his fine ones on Philips the
musician. Keep your promise, and let me have them. I
offer my very best compliments to Mrs. Garrick, and ever am
Your warm admirer and friend,
JAMES BOSWELL.
*From the " Journal of a Tour to the Hebrides."*

## DR. JOHNSON ON MARY QUEEN OF SCOTS

I here began to indulge old Scottish sentiments, and to
express a warm regret, that, by our Union with England, we
were no more ;—our independent kingdom was lost.—
JOHNSON. " Sir, never talk of your independency, who
could let your Queen remain twenty years in captivity, and
then be put to death, without even a pretence of justice,
without your ever attempting to rescue her ; and such a
Queen too ! as every man of any gallantry of spirit would
have sacrificed his life for."

*Idem.*

## HOLLY, GREEN HOLLY

Alone in greenwood must I roam,
  *Hollin, green hollin !*
A shade of green leaves is my home,
  *Birk & green hollin !*

Where nought is seen but boundless green,
  *Hollin, green hollin !*
And spots of far blue sky between,
  *Birk & green hollin !*

A weary head a pillow finds,
  *Hollin, green hollin !*
Where leaves fall green in summer winds,
  *Birk & green hollin !*

Enough for me, enough for me,
  *Hollin, green hollin !*
To live at large with liberty,
  *Birk & green hollin !*

  *Old Border Song.*

## INSCRIPTION IN MELROSE ABBEY

The earth goes on the earth glittering in gold,
  The earth goes to the earth sooner than it wold ;
The earth builds on the earth castles and towers,
  The earth says to the earth—All this is ours.

## A WET SHEET AND A FLOWING SEA

A wet sheet and a flowing sea,
  A wind that follows fast,
And fills the white and rustling sail,
  And bends the gallant mast—
And bends the gallant mast, my boys,
  While, like the eagle free,
Away the good ship flies, and leaves
  Old England on the lee.

O for a soft and gentle wind !
  I heard a fair one cry ;
But give to me the snoring breeze
  And white waves heaving high—
And white waves heaving high, my lads,
  The good ship tight and free ;
The world of waters is our home,
  And merry men are we.

There's tempest in yon hornèd moon,
  And lightning in yon cloud ;
And hark the music, mariners !
  The wind is piping loud—
The wind is piping loud, my boys,
  The lightning flashes free,
While the hollow oak our palace is,
  Our heritage the sea.

*Allan Cunningham* (1784-1842).


FRAGMENT

Gane were but the winter cauld,
  And gane were but the snaw,
I could sleep in the wild woods
  Where the primroses blaw.

*Idem.*

KILMENY

" *Having very little spare time from my flock, which was
unruly enough, I folded and stitched a few sheets of paper,
which I carried in my pocket. I had no inkhorn, but in place
of it I borrowed a small phial, which I fixed in a hole in the
breast of my waistcoat ; and having a cork fastened by a
piece of twine, it answered the purpose fully as well. Thus
equipped, whenever a leisure minute or two offered, and I had
nothing else to do, I sat down and wrote out my thoughts
as I found them.*"

*From the Autobiography of James Hogg.*

BONNIE Kilmeny gaed up the glen ;
But it wasna to meet Duneira's men,
Nor the rosy monk of the isle to see,
For Kilmeny was pure as pure could be.

206

It was only to hear the yorlin [1] sing,
And pu' the cress-flower round the spring;
The scarlet hypp and the hind-berrye,[2]
And the nut that hang frae the hazel tree;
For Kilmeny was pure as pure could be.
But lang may her minny [3] look o'er the wa';
And lang may she seek i' the green-wood shaw [4];
Lang the laird o' Duneira blame,
And lang, lang greet [5] or Kilmeny come hame!

When many a day had come and fled,
When grief grew calm, and hope was dead,
When mess for Kilmeny's soul had been sung,
When the bedesman had pray'd and the dead-bell
    rung,
Late, late in a gloamin when all was still,
When the fringe was red on the westlin hill,
The wood was sere, the moon i' the wane,
The reek [6] o' the cot hung over the plain,
Like a little wee cloud in the world its lane [7];
When the ingle lowed [8] wi' an eiry leme [9]—
Late, late in the gloamin Kilmeny came hame!

" Kilmeny, Kilmeny, where have you been?
Lang hae we sought baith holt and dean;
By linn, by ford, and green-wood tree,
Yet you are halesome and fair to see.

[1] Yellow-hammer.          [2] Wild raspberry.
[3] Mother.                 [4] Copse.
[5] Weep.                  [6] Smoke.
[7] By itself.            [8] Glowed.
[9] Eerie gleam.

Where gat ye that joup [1] o' the lily sheen ?
That bonnie snood [2] o' the birk sae green ?
And these roses, the fairest that ever were seen ?
Kilmeny, Kilmeny, where have you been ? "

Kilmeny look'd up wi' a lovely grace,
But nae smile was seen on Kilmeny's face ;
As still was her look, and as still was her e'e,
As the stillness that lay on the emerant lea,
Or the mist that sleeps on a waveless sea.
For Kilmeny had been, she knew not where,
And Kilmeny had seen what she could not declare ;
Kilmeny had been where the cock never crew,
Where the rain never fell, and the wind never blew.
But it seemed as the harp of the sky had rung,
And the airs of heaven played round her tongue,
When she spake of the lovely forms she had seen,
And a land where sin had never been ;
A land of love and a land of light,
Withouten sun, or moon, or night ;
Where the river swa'd [3] a living stream,
And the light a pure celestial beam ;
The land of vision, it would seem,
A still, an everlasting dream.

In yon green-wood there is a waik,[4]
And in that waik there is a wene,[5]
And in that wene there is a maike,[6]
That neither has flesh, blood, nor bane ;
And down in yon green-wood he walks his lane.[7]

[1] Petticoat.                      [2] Hair-band.
[3] Swelled.                        [4] Glade.
[5] Recess.                         [6] Mate.
                 [7] By himself.

208

In that green wene Kilmeny lay,
Her bosom happ'd wi' flowerets gay ;
But the air was soft and the silence deep,
And bonnie Kilmeny fell sound asleep.
She ken'd nae mair, nor open'd her e'e,
Till wak'd by the hymns of a far countrye.

She wakened on a couch of the silk sae slim,
All striped wi' the bars of the rainbow's rim ;
And lovely beings round were rife,
Who erst had travelled mortal life ;
And aye they smiled and 'gan to speer,[1]
" What spirit has brought this mortal here ? "

" Lang have I journey'd, the world wide,"
A meek and reverend fere [2] replied ;
" Baith night and day I have watched the fair,
Eident [3] a thousand years and mair.
Yes, I have watched o'er ilk degree,
Wherever blooms femenitye ;
But sinless virgin, free of stain
In mind and body, fand I nane.
Never, since the banquet of time,
Found I a virgin in her prime,
Till late this bonnie maiden I saw,
As spotless as the morning snaw ;
Full twenty years she has lived as free
As the spirits that sojourn in this countrye :
I have brought her away frae the snares of men,
That sin or death she never may ken."

[1] Ask.      [2] Companion.
    [3] Unrestingly.

They clasped her waist and her hands sae fair,
They kissed her cheek, and they kemed [1] her hair ;
And round came many a blooming fere,
Saying, " Bonnie Kilmeny, ye 're welcome here !
Women are freed of the littand [2] scorn ;
O blest be the day Kilmeny was born !
Now shall the land of the spirits see,
Now shall it ken what a woman may be !
Many a lang year, in sorrow and pain,
Many a lang year through the world we've gane,
Commissioned to watch fair womankind,
For it 's they who nurice the immortal mind.
We have watched their steps as the dawning shone,
And deep in the green-wood walks alone ;
By lily bower and silken bed,
The viewless tears have o'er them shed ;
Have soothed their ardent minds to sleep,
Or left the couch of love to weep.
We have seen ! we have seen ! but the time maun come,
And the angels will weep at the day of doom !

" O would the fairest of mortal kind
Aye keep the holy truths in mind,
That kindred spirits their motions see,
Who watch their ways with anxious e'e,
And grieve for the guilt of humanitye !
O, sweet to Heaven the maiden's prayer,
And the sigh that heaves a bosom sae fair !
And dear to Heaven the words of truth,
And the praise of virtue frae beauty's mouth !
And dear to the viewless forms of air,
The minds that kythe [3] as the body fair !

[1] Combed.          [2] Staining, defiling.          [3] Appear.

"O, bonnie Kilmeny! free frae stain,
If ever you seek the world again,
That world of sin, of sorrow, and fear,
O tell of the joys that are waiting here;
And tell of the signs you shall shortly see;
Of the times that are now, and the times that shall be."

They lifted Kilmeny, they led her away,
And she walked in the light of a sunless day;
The sky was a dome of crystal bright,
The fountain of vision, and fountain of light;
The emerald fields were of dazzling glow,
And the flowers of everlasting blow.
Then deep in the stream her body they laid,
That her youth and her beauty never might fade;
And they smil'd on Heaven, when they saw her lie
In the stream of life that wandered by.
And she heard a song, she heard it sung,
She ken'd not where; but sae sweetly it rung,
It fell on the ear like a dream of the morn;—
"O blest be the day Kilmeny was born!
Now shall the land of spirits see,
Now shall it ken what a woman may be!
The sun that shines on the world sae bright,
A borrowed gleid [1] frae the fountain of light;
And the moon that sleeks [2] the sky sae dun,
Like a gouden bow, or a beamless sun,
Shall wear away and be seen nae mair,
And the angels shall miss them travelling the air.
But lang, lang after baith nicht and day,
When the sun and the world have elyed [3] away;

[1] Spark.        [2] Makes smooth.        [3] Vanished.

P 2

When the sinner has gane to his waesome doom,
Kilmeny shall smile in eternal bloom ! "—

They bore her away, she wist not how,
For she felt not arm nor rest below ;
But so swift they wained [1] her through the light,
'Twas like the motion of sound or sight ;
They seemed to split the gales of air,
And yet nor gale nor breeze was there.
Unnumbered groves below them grew,
They came, they pass'd, and backward flew,
Like floods of blossoms gliding on,
In moment seen, in moment gone.
O, never vales to mortal view
Appeared like those o'er which they flew !
That land to human spirits given,
The lowermost vales of the storied heaven ;
From thence they can view the world below,
And heaven's blue gates with sapphires glow,
More glory yet unmeet to know.

They bore her far to a mountain green,
To see what mortal never had seen ;
And they seated her high on a purple sward,
And bade her heed what she saw and heard,
And note the changes the spirits wrought,
For now she lived in the land of thought.
She looked, and she saw nor sun nor skies,
But a crystal dome of a thousand dyes :
She looked, and she saw nae land aright,
But an endless whirl of glory and light ;

[1] Carried.

212

And radiant beings went and came,
Far swifter than wind, or the linkèd flame.
She hid her een frae the dazzling view ;
She looked again, and the scene was new.

She saw a sun in a summer sky,
And clouds of amber sailing by ;
A lovely land beneath her lay,
And that land had glens and mountains grey ;
And that land had valleys and hoary piles,
And marled ¹ seas and a thousand isles :
Its fields were speckled, its forests green,
And its lakes were all of the dazzling sheen,
Like magic mirrors, where slumbering lay
The sun, and the sky, and the cloudlet grey ;
Which heaved and trembled, and gently swung,
On every shore they seemed to be hung :
For there they were seen on their downward plain
A thousand times and a thousand again ;
In winding lake, and placid firth,
Like peaceful heavens in the bosom of earth.

Kilmeny sighed and seemed to grieve,
For she found her heart to that land did cleave ;
She saw the corn wave on the vale ;
She saw the deer run down the dale ;
She saw the plaid and the broad claymore,
And the brows that the badge of freedom bore ;
And she thought she had seen the land before.

She saw a lady sit on a throne,
The fairest that ever the sun shone on !

¹ Variegated.

213

A lion licked her hand of milk,
And she held him in a leish of silk ;
And a leifu' [1] maiden stood at her knee,
With a silver wand and melting e'e ;
Her sovereign shield till love stole in,
And poisoned all the fount within.

Then a gruff untoward bedesman came,
And hundit the lion on his dame ;
And the guardian maid wi' the dauntless e'e,
She dropped a tear, and left her knee ;
And she saw till the queen frae the lion fled,
Till the bonniest flower o' the world lay dead ;
A coffin was set on a distant plain,
And she saw the red blood fall like rain ;
Then bonnie Kilmeny's heart grew sair,
And she turned away, and could look nae mair.

Then the gruff grim carle girned [2] amain,
And they trampled him down, but he rose again ;
And he baited the lion to deeds of weir,[3]
Till he lapp'd the blood to the kingdom dear ;
And weening his head was danger-preef,[4]
When crowned with the rose and clover leaf,
He gowl'd [5] at the carle, and chased him away
To feed wi' the deer on the mountain grey.
He gowl'd at the carle, and geck'd [6] at heaven,
But his mark was set, and his arles [7] given.
Kilmeny a while her een withdrew ;
She looked again, and the scene was new.

[1] Wistful.                         [2] Grinned.
[3] War.                             [4] Proof.
[5] Growled.                         [6] Mocked.
               [7] Earnest-money.

She saw before her fair unfurl'd
One half of all the glowing world,
Where oceans rolled, and rivers ran,
To bound the aims of sinful man.
She saw a people, fierce and fell,
Burst frae their bounds like fiends of hell;
There lilies grew, and the eagle flew ;
And she herkèd [1] on her ravening crew,
Till the cities and towers were wrapt in a blaze,
And the thunder it roared o'er the lands and the seas.
The widows they wailed, and the red blood ran,
And she threatened an end to the race of man ;
She never lened,[2] nor stood in awe,
Till caught by the lion's deadly paw,
O, then the eagle swinked [3] for life,
And brainzelled up [4] a mortal strife ;
But she flew north, or flew she south,
She met wi' the gowl o' the lion's mouth.

With a mooted [5] wing and waefu' maen,
The eagle sought her eiry again ;
But lang may she cower in her bloody nest,
And lang, lang sleek her wounded breast,
Before she sey [6] another flight,
To play wi' the norland lion's might.

But to sing the sights Kilmeny saw,
So far surpassing nature's law,
The singer's voice wad sink away,
And the string of his harp wad cease to play.

[1] Hounded.                    [2] Crouched.
[3] Struggled.                  [4] Caused to break out.
[5] Moulted, draggled.          [6] Essay.

But she saw till the sorrows of man were by,
And all was love and harmony ;
Till the stars of heaven fell calmly away,
Like flakes of snaw on a winter day.

Then Kilmeny begged again to see
The friends she had left in her own countrye,
To tell of the place where she had been,
And the glories that lay in the land unseen ;
To warn the living maidens fair,
The loved of Heaven, the spirits' care,
That all whose minds unmeled [1] remain
Shall bloom in beauty when time is gane.

With distant music, soft and deep,
They lulled Kilmeny sound asleep ;
And when she awakened, she lay her lane, [2]
All happ'd with flowers, in the green-wood wene.
When seven lang years had come and fled,
When grief was calm, and hope was dead ;
When scarce was remembered Kilmeny's name,
Late, late in a gloamin Kilmeny came hame.
And O, her beauty was fair to see,
But still and steadfast was her e'e !
Such beauty bard may never declare,
For there was no pride nor passion there ;
And the soft desire of maiden's een
In that mild face could never be seen.
Her seymar [3] was the lily flower,
And her cheek the moss-rose in the shower ;
And her voice like the distant melodye,

[1] Unmixed, pure.                [2] By herself.
          [3] Loose robe.

216

That floats along the twilight sea,
But she loved to raike [1] the lanely glen,
And keeped afar frae the haunts of men ;
Her holy hymns unheard to sing,
To suck the flowers, and drink the spring :
But wherever her peaceful form appeared,
The wild beasts of the hill were cheered ;
The wolf played blythely round the field,
The lordly byson lowed, and kneeled ;
The dun deer wooed with manner bland,
And cowered aneath her lily hand.
And when at eve the woodlands rung,
When hymns of other worlds she sung
In ecstasy of sweet devotion,
O, then the glen was all in motion !
The wild beasts of the forest came,
Broke from their bughts [2] and faulds the tame,
And goved [3] around, charmed and amazed ;
Even the dull cattle crooned and gazed,
And murmured, and looked with anxious pain
For something the mystery to explain.
The buzzard came with the throstle-cock ;
The corby left her houf [4] in the rock ;
The blackbird alang wi' the eagle flew ;
The hind came tripping o'er the dew ;
The wolf and the kid their raike [5] began,
And the tod, [6] and the lamb, and the leveret ran ;
The hawk and the hern attour them hung,
And the merle and the mavis forhooyed their young ;

[1] Range.                    [2] Pens.
[3] Stared.                   [4] Haunt.
[5] Ramble.                   [6] Fox.

217

And all in a peaceful ring were hurled ;
It was like an eve in a sinless world !

When a month and a day had come and gane,
Kilmeny sought the green-wood wene ;
There laid her down on the leaves sae green,
And Kilmeny on earth was never mair seen.
But O ! the words that fell frae her mouth
Were words of wonder, and words of truth !
But all the land were in fear and dread,
For they kendna whether she was living or dead.
It wasna her hame, and she couldna remain ;
She left this world of sorrow and pain,
And returned to the land of thought again.

*James Hogg* (1770–1835).

### FOUR SCOTTISH TOASTS

1. May the hinges of friendship ne'er rust, or the wings of love lose a feather.

2. When we are going up the hill of fortune may we ne'er meet a friend coming down.

3. May the winds of adversity ne'er blow open our door.

4. May the mouse ne'er leave our meal pock with the tear in its eye.

### THE WIT OF ONE, AND THE WISDOM OF MANY

*Parœmia est celebre dictum scitâ quâpiam novitate insigne.*
*Erasmus.*

1. A proud heart in a poor breast has meikle dolour to dree.

2. All keys in the country hang not at ane belt.

218

3. An ounce of mother's wit is worth a pound of clergy.
4. It is dear bought honey that's licked off a thorn.
5. Kings and bears oft worry their keepers.
6. The day hath eyes, the night hath ears.
7. A change o'deils is lichtsome.
8. Hang a thief when he's young, and he'll no steal when he's old.
9. The King's errand may come to the cadger's gate yet.
10. He that teaches himself has a fool for his master.
11. A Scots mist will wet an Englishman to the skin.
12. The evening brings all hame.[1]

[1] The literal idea of this old proverb has a high and illustrious antiquity as in the fragment of Sappho : Ἑσπέρε, παντα φερεις—φέρεις ὄιν, φέρεις αῖγα φέρεις μάτερι παῖδα.

# PART V

I love a ballad in print o' life,
For then we are sure they are true.

*Shakespeare " Winter's Tale," IV.*, 4, 255.

I knew a very wise man who believed that if a man were
permitted to make all the ballads, he need not care who
should make the laws of the nation.

*Andrew Fletcher of Saltoun* (1658-1716).

A ballad, then, of love and dreadful Death ;
For sorrow feeds upon my heart,
And I am weary of a dancing measure.

*Anon.*

" Say, O Fool ! which is the heavier and more grievous
burden—the trials of love, or the trials of such as love not ? "
And he answered : " Go, enquire of those that do penance
for the love of their Beloved, and of those that do penance
from fear of the pains of Hell."

*From " The Book of the Lover and the Beloved,"*
*Ramon Lull (c.* 1285).

221

# THE LAMENT OF THE QUEEN OF ELFLAND'S NOURICE

*The Queen of Elfland had spirited away a human mother to be her child's nurse, beyond the rim of the world. And because of the enchantments laid upon her, this woman forgot her own country and the little son that she had left when he was only " four nights " old. But one day, hearing a cow lowing for its calf, she remembered as in a dream . . . and, sick at heart, roused her mistress and begged for permission to return to the " Christian land " wherein she used to dwell. The Queen, although she pointed out the road to earth, refused to release her until the child could walk alone. An old superstition tells us that women were often enticed, when in childbed, to nurse fairy children, " a lingering voracious image of them being substituted, like their reflection in a mirror, or some insatiable spirit in an assumed body."*

> *" I heard a cow low, a bonnie cow low,*
> *And a cow low down in yon glen :*
> *Lang, lang will my young son greet,*
> *Or his mither bid him come ben !* [1]
>
> *I heard a cow low, a bonnie cow low,*
> *And a cow low down in yon fauld :*
> *Lang, lang will my young son greet,*
> *Or his mither shield him frae cauld !* " . . .

The Queen of Elfan's nourice
She sits and sings her lane
" Waken, Queen of Elfan,
And hear your nourice moan."

[1] In.

" O moan ye for your meat ?
Or moan ye for your fee ?
Or moan ye for the ither bounties
That ladies are wont to gie ? "

" I moan not for my meat,
I moan not for my fee ;
But I moan for my Christian land
It's there I fain would be.

For I heard a bonnie cow low
Low down in yonder fauld
And I mind me of my little son
I left in four nights auld." . . .

" O nurse my bairn, nourice,
Till he stand at your knee,
An ye's win hame to Christian land
Whar fain it's ye wad be.

O keep my bairn, nourice,
Till he gang by the hauld,[1]
An ye's win hame to your young son
Ye left in four nights auld.

O nourice, lay your head
Here upon my knee :
See ye not that narrow road
Up by yonder tree ?

See ye not the narrow road
By yonder lillie leven ? [2]
That's the road the righteous goes
And that's the road to Heaven.

[1] Until he can walk hand in hand with somebody.
[2] Lily lawn.

An see ye not that braid road
Down by yon sunny fell ?
Yon's the road the wicked gae ?
An that's the road to Hell.

An see ye not that bonny road
About the fernie brae ?
That wins back free Elfland
Where ye must wait to gae."

## FRAGMENT

*In this we catch a fleeting glimpse of an unseemly lady who,
one still evening, beguiled and murdered her " own true love,"
and who, in dreadful apprehension of the consequences of this
evil deed, turns now this way, now that, to save herself. But
although she tries to bribe her wily parrot with a cage of beaten
gold, and her bower-maiden with the shimmering silks which
were to have made her own new Easter gown, she is condemned
to go where there will be " no floating dust, no scent, no twilight,
no twinkling of the stars." . . . And so the angry flames of a
hurriedly lit bonfire destroyed those " false false arms in which
poor young Redin lay."*

O ! lang, lang, is the winter nicht,
And slowly dawns the day ;
There is a slain knight in my bower,
And I wish he were away.

Then up bespak her bower-woman,
And she spak ae wi' spite :
" An there be a slain knicht in your bower
It's yourself that has the wyte." [1]

[1] Blame.

" O heal [1] this deed on me, Meggy,
O heal this deed on me,
The silks that were shapen for me gen Pasche [2]
Thay shal be sewed for thee."

Then up bespak the wylie parrot,
As he sat on the tree,—
" And hae ye kill'd young Redin
Wha ne'er had love but thee ! "

" Come down, come down, ye wylie parrot,
Come down into my hand ;
Your cage shal be of beaten gold
When now it's but the wand." [3]

" I winna come down, I canna come down,
I winna come down to thee ;
For as ye've done to young Redin,
Ye'll do the like to me."

## THE CRUEL BROTHER OR THE BRIDE'S TESTAMENT

*This is a tragic tale over which a revengeful brother casts a sinister shadow. The closing bequest of the dying bride to her innocent sister-in-law : " The wilderness to end her life " is like the echo of another ballad of Nemesis, " Son Davie," in which " The weary world to wander up and down " is the grim legacy in the last verse.*

There was three ladies played at the ba,
*With a hey ho and a lillie gay.*

There came a Knight and played o'er them a'
*As the primrose spreads so sweetly.*

[1] Hide.  [2] Easter.  [3] Wicker.

226

The eldest was baith tall and fair,
But the youngest was beyond compare.

The midmost had a graceful mien,
But the youngest looked like beautie's queen.

The Knight bowed low to a' the three,
But to the youngest he bent his knee.

The ladie turned her head aside,
The Knight he wooed her to be his bride.

The ladie blushed a rosy red
And sayd : " Sir Knight, I'm too young to wed."

" O ladie fair, give me your hand
And I'll mak you ladie of a' my land."

" Sir Knight, ere ye my favor win
You maun get consent frae a' my kin.

He's got consent frae her parents dear
And likewise frae her sisters fair.

He's got consent frae her kin each one
But forgot to spiek to her brother John.

Now when the wedding day was come
The Knight would take his bonny bride home.

And many a lord and many a Knight
Came to behold that ladie bright.

And there was nae man that did her see
But wish'd himself bridegroom to be.

Her father dear led her down the stair
And her sisters twain they kissed her there.

Her mother dear led her through the close
And her brother John set her on her horse.

She lean'd her o'er the saddle bow,
To give him a kiss ere she did go.

He has ta'en a knife baith lang and sharp
And stabb'd that bonny bride to the heart.

She had no ridden half thro' the town
Until her heart's blude stained her gown.

" Ride softly on," says the best young man,
" For I think our bonny bride looks pale and wan."

" O lead me gently up yon hill,
And I'll there sit down and make my will."

" O what will you leave to your father dear ? "
" The silver shode steed that brought me here."

" What will you leave to your mother dear ? "
" My velvet pall and my silken gear."

" What will you leave to your sister Anne ? "
" My silken scarf and my gowden fan."

" What will you leave to your sister Grace ? "
" My bloody cloaths to wash and dress."

" What will you leave to your brother John ? "
" The gallows tree to hang him on."

" What will you leave to your brother John's wife ? "
" The wilderness to end her life."

This lady fair in her grave was laid
And many a mass was o'er her said.

But it would have made your heart right sair
To see the bridegroom rive his haire.

## SIR JOHN SUCKLING'S CAMPAIGNE

*When the Scottish covenanters rose up in arms, and advanced to the English borders in 1639, many of the courtiers complimented the king by raising forces at their own expense. Among these none was more distinguished than the gallant Sir John Suckling, a great favourite with Charles I., who raised a troop of horse, so richly accoutred, in their scarlet coats and white doublets, that it cost him £12,000. The expensive equipment of other parts of the army, too, made the king remark, that " the Scots would fight stoutly, if it were but for the Englishmen's fine cloaths." When they came to action, the rugged Scots proved more than a match for the fine showy English ; many of whom behaved remarkably ill, and among the rest this splendid troop of Sir John Suckling's. The following pasquil is supposed to have been written by Sir John, as a banter upon himself.*

Sir John he got him an ambling nag,
   To Scotland for to ride-a,
With a hundred horse more, all his own he swore,
   To guard him on every side-a.


No Errant-knight ever went to fight,
   With half so gay a bravada,
Had you seen but his look, you'ld have sworn on a book,
   Hee'ld have conquer'd a whole armada.


The ladies ran all to the windows to see
   So gallant and warlike a sight-a,
And as he pass'd by, they said with a sigh,
   Sir John, why will you go fight-a ?

But he, like a cruel knight, spurr'd on ;
  His heart would not relent-a,
For, till he came there, what had he to fear ?
  Or why should he repent-a ?

The king (God bless him !) had singular hopes
  Of him and all his troop-a :
The borderers they, as they met him on the way,
  For joy did hallow, and whoop-a.

None lik'd him so well, as his own colonell,
  Who took him for John de Wert-a ; [1]
But when there were shows of gunning and blows,
  My gallant was nothing so pert-a.

For when the Scots army came within sight,
  And all prepared to fight-a,
He ran to his tent, they ask'd what he meant,
  He swore he must needs goe sleep-a.

The colonell sent for him back agen,
  To quarter him in the van-a,
But Sir John did swear, he would not come there,
  To be kill'd the very first man-a.

To cure his fear, he was sent to the reare,
  Some ten miles back, and more-a,
Where Sir John did play at trip and away,
  And ne'er saw the enemy more-a.

---

[1] John de Wert was a German general of great reputation, and the
terror of the French in the reign of Louis XIII. Hence his name became
proverbial in France, where he was called De Vert.

## THE FALSE KNIGHT UPON THE ROAD

*It was said that the Devil had power to carry off any traveller who was unable to give good answers to his questions. In this ballad we find a youth who kept his wits and in each case " had the last word."*

" O whare are ye gaun ? "
  *Quo' the fause knicht* [1] *upon the road :*
" I'm gaun to the scule,"
  *Quo' the wee boy, and still he stude.*

" What is that upon your back ? "
  *Quo' the fause knicht upon the road :*
" Atweel it is my bukes,"
  *Quo' the wee boy, and still he stude.*

" What's that ye've got in your arm ? "
  *Quo' the fause knicht upon the road :*
" Atweel it is my peit," [2]
  *Quo' the wee boy, and still he stude.*

" Wha's aucht thae sheep ? "
  *Quo' the fause knicht upon the road :*
" They are mine and my mither's,"
  *Quo' the wee boy, and still he stude.*

" How mony o' them are mine ? "
  *Quo' the fause knicht upon the road :*
" A' they that hae blue tails,"
  *Quo' the wee boy, and still he stude.*

[1] The Devil.
[2] Peat as a gift for the schoolmaster.

" I wiss ye were on yon tree,"
*Quo' the fause knicht upon the road :*
" And a gude ladder under me,"
*Quo' the wee boy, and still he stude.*

" And the ladder for to break,"
*Quo' the fause knicht upon the road :*
" And you for to fa' down,"
*Quo' the wee boy, and still he stude.*

" I wiss ye were in yon sie,"
*Quo' the fause knicht upon the road :*
" And a gude bottom [1] under me,"
*Quo' the wee boy, and still he stude.*

" And the bottom for to break,"
*Quo' the fause knicht upon the road :*
" And ye to be drowned,"
*Quo' the wee boy, and still he stude.*

### THERE WAS A KNIGHT

*In this ballad the Devil disguised as a Knight comes to the house of a widow to woo her daughters, but the youngest one, Jennifer, " bold and bright," proved to be too clever for him, and answered all his questions, until, quite overcome, " he flew awa' in a blazing flame."*

There was a knicht riding frae the east,
*Jennifer gentle an' rosemaree.*
Who had been wooing at monie a place,
*As the doo [2] flies owre the mulberry tree.*

[1] *Bottom*, ship.          [2] Dove.

He cam' unto a widow's door,
And speird [1] whare her three dochters were.

" The auldest ane's to a washing gane,
The second's to a baking gane.

" The youngest ane's to a wedding gane,
And it will be nicht or [2] she be hame."

He sat him doun upon a stane,
Till thir three lasses cam' tripping hame.

The auldest ane she let him in,
And pinned the door wi' a siller pin.

The second ane she made his bed,
And laid saft pillows unto his head.

The youngest ane was bauld [3] and bricht,
And she tarried for words wi' this unco knicht.—

" Gin ye will answer me questions ten,
The morn ye sall be made my ain :—

" O what is higher nor [4] the tree ?
And what is deeper nor the sea ?

" Or what is heavier nor the lead ?
And what is better nor the bread ?

" Or what is whiter nor the milk ?
Or what is safter nor the silk ?

" Or what is sharper nor a thorn ?
Or what is louder nor a horn ? "

[1] Asked.          [2] Ere.
[3] Bold.          [4] Than.

" O heaven is higher nor the tree,
And hell is deeper nor the sea—

" O sin is heavier nor the lead
The blessing's better nor the bread.

" The snaw is whiter nor the milk,
And the down is softer nor the silk.

" Hunger is sharper nor a thorn,
And shame is louder nor a horn.

" The pies are greener nor the grass,
And Clootie's [1] worse than a woman was."

As soon as she the fiend did name,
*Jennifer gentle an' rosemaree,*
He flew awa' in a blazing flame,
*As the doo flies owre the mulberry tree.*


### THE YOUNG MAXWELL

*This ballad is founded on fact. A young member of the family of Maxwell, seeing his paternal house reduced to ashes, and all his relatives killed, assumed the habit of an old shepherd, singled out one of the men who had ruined his home, and slew him in single combat.*

" O whare gang ye, thou silly auld carle ? [2]
And what do ye carry there ? "
" I'm gaun to the hill side, thou sodger man,
To shift my sheep their lair."

[1] Clootie's Croft is a piece of wild untilled land, which the superstitious handed over in name to the Devil in the hopes of propitiating him.
[2] *I.e.,* old man.

Ae stride or twa took the silly auld carle,
And a gude lang stride took he ;
" I trow thou be a feck auld carle ;
Will you shaw the way to me ? "

And he is gane wi' the silly auld carle
Adown by the greenwood side :
" Light down and gang, thou sodger man,
For here ye canna ride."

He drew the reins o' his bonny grey stead,
And lightly down he sprang :
Of the comeliest scarlet was his weir-coat,
Whare the gowden tassels hang.

He has thrawn aff his plaid, the silly auld carle,
And his bonnet frae 'boon his bree,
And wha was it but the young Maxwell !
And his gude brown sword drew he.

" Thou kill'd my father, thou vile Southron,
And thou kill'd my brethren three,
Whilk brak the heart o' my ae sister,
I lov'd as the light o' my e'e.

" Draw out your sword, thou vile Southron,
Red wat wi' blude o' my kin ;
That sword it crappit [1] the bonniest flower
E'er lifted its head to the sun.

" There's ae sad stroke for my dear auld father,
There's twa for my brethren three,
And there's ane to thy heart for my ae sister,
Wham I lov'd as the light o' my e'e."

[1] Cropped.

235

## YOUNG WATERS

*It is thought that this ballad alludes to the partiality of Queen Anne of Denmark for the Bonny Earl of Murray, who was " cruelly murthered in 1592 by the Earle of Huntley to satisfie the King's jealousie."*

About Zule,[1] quhen the wind blew cule,
    And the round tables began,
A' ! there is cum to our kings court
    Mony a well-favour'd man.

The queen luikt owre the castle wa,
    Beheld baith dale and down,
And then she saw zoung Waters
    Cum riding to the town.

His footmen they did rin before,
    His horsemen rade behind,
Ane mantel of the burning gowd [2]
    Did keip him frae the wind.

Gowden graith'd [3] his horse before
    And siller shod behind,
The horse zong Waters rade upon
    Was fleeter than the wind.

But than spake a wylie lord,
    Unto the queen said he,
O tell me qhua's the fairest face
    Rides in the company.

[1] Christmas.      [2] Gold.      [3] Golden-accoutred.

I've sene lord, and I've sene laird,
    And knights of high degree ;
Bot a fairer face than zoung Watèrs,
    Mine eyne did never see.

Out then spack the jealous king,
    (And an angry man was he)
O' if he had been twice as fair,
    Zou micht have excepted me.

Zou're neither laird nor lord, she says,
    But the king that wears the crown ;
Theris not a knight in fair Scotland
    Bot to thee maun bow down.

For a' that she could do or say,
    Appeas'd he wad nae bee ;
Bot for the words which she had said
    Zoung Waters he maun dee.

They hae taen zoung Waters, and
    Put fetters to his feet ;
They hae taen zoung Waters, and
    Thrown him in dungeon deep.

Aft I have ridden thro' Stirling town
    In the wind both and the weit ;
Bot I neir rade thro' Stirling town
    Wi fetters at my feet.

Aft have I ridden thro' Stirling town
    In the wind both and the rain ;
Bot I neir rade thro' Stirling town
    Neir to return again.

They hae taen to the heiding-hill [1]
His zoung son in his craddle,
And they hae taen to the heiding-hill
His horse both and his saddle.

They hae taen to the heiding-hill
His lady fair to see.
And for the words the Queene had spoke
Zoung Waters he did dee.

## THE MURDER OF THE KING OF SCOTS

*The subject of this Ballad, written in 1568, is the murder of Henry Lord Darnley, great-nephew of Henry VIII., and husband of Mary Queen of Scots. Although the eulogium bestowed upon him in the first verse is somewhat extravagant, he is said to have had such charm that Mary " was stricken with the dart of love by the comeliness of his sweet behaviour, personage, wit, vertuous qualities, languages and lettered sciences, as also in the art of music, dancing, and playing instruments." By this union she strengthened her position as the heir-presumptive to the throne of England, for it was in virtue of his father's claims as the grandson of Margaret Tudor, as well as of his mother's rights, that James VI. obtained the English throne in 1603.*

Woe worth, woe worth thee, false Scotlànde !
For thou hast ever wrought by sleight ;
The worthyest prince that ever was borne,
You hanged under a cloud by night.

[1] Beheading.

238

The queene of France a letter wrote,
   And sealed itt with harte and ringe ;
And bade him come Scotland within,
   And shee wold marry and crowne him kinge.

To be a king is a pleasant thing,
   To bee a prince unto a peere :
But you have heard, and soe have I too,
   A man may well buy gold too deare.

There was an Italyan in that place,
   Was as well beloved as ever was hee,
Lord David [1] was his name,
   Chamberlaine to the queene was hee.

If the king had risen forth of his place,
   He wold have sate him downe in the cheare,
And tho itt beseemed him not so well,
   Altho the kinge had been present there.

Some lords in Scotlande waxed wroth,
   And quarrelled with him for the nonce ;
I shall you tell how it befell,
   Twelve daggers were in him att once.

When the queene saw her chamberlaine was slaine,
   For him her faire cheeks shee did weete,
And made a vowe for a yeare and a day
   The king and shee wold not come in one sheete.

Then some of the lords they waxed wrothe,
   And made their vow all vehementlye ;
For the death of the queenes chamberlaine,
   The king himselfe, how he shall dye.

[1] *I.e.*, Rizzio.

239

With gun-powder they strewed his roome,
    And lay'd greene rushes in his way :
For the traitors thought that very night
    This worthye king for to betray.

To bedd the king he made him bowne ;
    To take his rest was his desire ;
He was noe sooner cast on sleepe,
    But his chamber was on a blasing fire.

Up he lope, and the window brake,
    And hee had thirtye foote to fall ;
Lord Bodwell kept a privy watch,
    Underneath his castle wall.

Who have wee here ?  Lord Bodwell sayd :
    Now answer me, that I may know.
" King Henry the Eighth my uncle was ;
    For his sweete sake some pitty show."

Who have we here ?  Lord Bodwell sayd,
    Now answer me when I doe speake.
" Ah, lord Bodwell, I know thee well ;
    Some pitty on me I pray thee take."

Ile pitty thee as much, he sayd,
    And as much favor show to thee,
As thou didst to the queenes chamberlaine,
    That day thou deemedst him to die.

Through halls and towers the king they ledd,
    Through towers and castles that were nye,
Through an arbor into an orchàrd,
    There on a peare-tree hanged him hye.

When the governor of Scotland heard
How that the worthye king was slaine ;
He persued the queen so bitterlye,
That in Scotland shee dare not remaine.

But she is fledd into merry England,[1]
And here her residence hath taine ;
And through the queene of Englands grace,
In England now shee doth remaine.

### FINE FLOWERS IN THE VALLEY

*This beautiful fragment is also known as " The Cruel
Mother " or " Lady Anne."*

She sat down below a thorn,
   *Fine flowers in the valley ;*
And there she has her sweet babe born,
   *And the green leaves they grow rarely.*

" Smile na sae sweet, my bonny babe,
   *Fine flowers in the valley,*
And ye smile sae sweet, ye'll smile me dead,"
   *And the green leaves they grow rarely.*

She's ta'en out her little penknife,
   *Fine flowers in the valley,*
And twinn'd the sweet babe o' its life,
   *And the green leaves they grow rarely.*

She's howket a grave by the light o' the moon,
   *Fine flowers in the valley,*
And there she's buried her sweet babe in,
   *And the green leaves they grow rarely.*

[1] *I.e.,* in 1568.

As she was going to the church,
*Fine flowers in the valley,*
She saw a sweet babe in the porch,
*And the green leaves they grow rarely.*

" O sweet babe, and thou were mine,
*Fine flowers in the valley,*
I wad clead thee in the silk so fine,"
*And the green leaves they grow rarely.*

" O mother dear, when I was thine,
*Fine flowers in the valley,*
Ye did na prove to me sae kind,"
*And the green leaves they grow rarely.*


## LADY ISABEL AND THE ELF-KNIGHT

*This ballad has a wide circulation in the south as well as in the north of Europe. Some suggest that it is an offshoot of the tale of Judith and Holofernes, but it is in all probability imaginary. The inhabitants of the Fairy-world were, it seems, continually endeavouring to have contact with humanity, even as ghosts of the dead came harking back along the way they had passed. " In olde days . . .*
*Al was this land fulfilled of fayrie ;*
*The elf-queen, with hir joly compaignye,*
*Daunced full oft in many a grene mede."*

Fair Lady Isabel sits in her bower sewing,
*Aye as the gowans [1] grow gay ;*
There she heard an elf-knight blawing his horn,
*The first morning in May.*

[1] Daisies.

242

" If I had yon horn that I hear blawing,
And yon elf-knight to sleep in my bosom."

This maiden had scarcely these words spoken,
Till in at her window the elf-knight has luppen.

" It's a very strange matter, fair maiden," said he,
" I canna blaw my horn, but ye call on me."

" But will ye go to yon greenwood side,
If ye canna' gang, I will cause you to ride."

He leapt on a horse, and she on another,
And they rode on to the greenwood together.

" Light down, light down, Lady Isabel," said he,
" We are come to the place where ye are to die."

" Hae mercy, hae mercy, kind sir, on me,
Till ance my dear father and mother I see."

" Seven kings' daughters here hae I slain,
And ye shall be the eight o' them."

" O sit down a while, lay your head on my knee,
That we may hae some rest before that I die."

She strok'd him sae fast, the nearer he did creep,
Wi' a sma' charm she lull'd him fast asleep.

Wi' his ain sword belt sae fast as she ban' him,
With his ain dag-dirk sae sair as she dang him.

" If seven kings' daughters here ye ha'e slain,
Lie ye here, a husband to them a'."

### THE DEMON LOVER

" O whar hae ye been, my lang, lang love,
    These seven years past an' more ? "
" O I am come to mind ye o' the vows
    Ye granted me before."

" Now hald your tongue o' former vows,
    For they wad cause sad strife ;
O hald your tongue o' former vows,
    For I hae become a wife." [1]

He turn'd him right and roun' about,
    And tears blinded his e'e :
" I wad never hae trodden yon Irish groun'
    If it had not been for thee.

" I micht hae had a king's daughtèr,
    Far, far beyont the sea ;
I micht hae had a king's daughtèr,
    Had I ne'er lovèd thee."

" An' if ye had nae king's daughtèr
    Your sel ye had to blame ;
Ye micht hae taen the king's daughtèr,
    For ye ken'd that I was nane."

" O fause, fause vows o' womankind,
    An' fause is their fair bodiè !
I'd never hae trodden on Irish groun',
    But for the love o' thee."

[1] *The heroine of this ballad is supposed to have been Jane Reynolds, the wife of an Aberdeen ship's carpenter, and here carried off by the spirit of her previous lover. There are various seventeenth century tales with similar plots, but this is the only instance I have found of the dual personality of Satan and a sailor.*

244

" If I war to leave my husband dear
  And my twa babes also,
O whar hast thou to tak me to ?—
  If with thee I shuld go."

" I hae seven ships upo' the sea ;
  The eighth brought me to land,
Wi' four-an'-twenty brave marinèrs,
  An' music on ev'ry hand."

She has taken up her two little babes,
  Kiss'd them baith cheek and chin ;
" O fair ye weel, my ain two babes,
  For I'll never see you again."

She set her foot upon the ship,
  No mariners could she behold ;
But the sails were o' the taffety,
  And the masts o' the beaten gold.

She had not sail'd a league, a league,
  A league but barely three,
When dismal grew his countenance,
  And drumlie [1] grew his ee.

The masts that were like the beaten gold,
  Bent not on the heaving seas ;
But the sails, that were o' the taffety,
  Fill'd not in the east land-breeze.

They had not sailed a league, a league,
  A league but barely three,
Until she espied his cloven foot,
  And she wept right bitterly.

[1] Troubled.

245

" O hold your tongue of your weeping," says he,
  " Of your weeping now let me be ;
I will show you how the lilies grow
  On the banks of Italy."—

" O what hills are yon, yon pleasant hills,
  That the sun shines sweetly on ? "—
" O yon are the hills of heaven," he said,
  " Where you will never win."—

" O whaten a mountain is yon," she said,
  " All so dreary wi' frost and snow ? "
" O yon is the mountain of hell," he cried,
  " Where you and I will go."

And aye when she turn'd her round about,
  Aye taller he seem'd for to be ;
Until that the tops o' that gallant ship
  Nae taller were than he.

The clouds grew dark, and the wind grew loud,
  And the levin [1] fill'd her ee ;
And waesome wail'd the snaw-white sprites
  Upon the gurlie [2] sea.

He strack the tap-mast wi' his hand,
  The fore-mast wi' his knee ;
And he brake that gallant ship in twain,
  And sank her in the sea.

## THE MERMAID

*In her dwelling and in her appearance, the lovely fatal
mermaid of northern nations resembled the syrens of the ancients.*

[1] Lightning.        [2] Stormy.

*The appendages of a comb and mirror were probably of Celtic origin. The Kelpie was a malignant spirit of the waters in the form of a horse, and the sound of its malevolent neighing was said to be a boding of death to the unfortunate traveller.*

To yon fause stream that, by the sea,
    Hides mony an elf and plum,[1]
And rives wi' fearful din the stanes,
    A witless knicht did come.

The day shines clear : Far in he's gane,
    Whar shells are silver bright ;
Fishes war loupin' a' aroun'
    An' sparklin' to the light.

When, as he laved, sounds came sae sweet
    Frae ilka rock ajee [2] :
The brief was out ; 'twas him it doomed
    The mermaid's face to see.

Frae 'neath a rock sune, sune she rose,
    An' stately on she swam,
Stopped i' the midst, and becked and sang
    For him to stretch his han'.

Gowden glist the yellow links
    That roun' her neck she'd twine ;
Her een war o' the skyie blue,
    Her lips did mock the wine.

The smile upon her bonnie cheek
    Was sweeter than the bee ;
Her voice excell'd the birdie's sang
    Upon the birchen tree.

[1] Pool.    [2] On one side.

Sae couthie,[1] couthie did she look,
  And meikle had she fleeched [2] ;
Out shot his hand—alas ! alas !
  Fast in the swirl he screeched.

The mermaid leuched [3] ; her brief was dane ;
  The kelpie's blast was blawin' :
Fu' low she dived, ne'er cam' again ;
  For deep, deep was the fawin'.[4]

Aboon the stream his wraith was seen :
  Warlocks [5] tirl'd lang at gloamin' :
That e'en was coarse ; the blast blew hoarse
  Ere lang the waves war foamin'.

### BESSIE BELL AND MARY GRAY

*The mournful tale is that these two young ladies, natives of Perth, retired together to a rural retreat, where they built a bower, in the hopes of avoiding the plague of 1665. Notwithstanding this precaution, they both died of it. Thus, they were not buried " among their noble kin " ; but their bodies lay lonely and uncoffined in Dornock Hough—a green watermeadow—there " to bask beneath the sun."*

O Bessie Bell and Mary Gray,
  They war twa bonnie lasses ;
They biggit [6] a bower on yon Burn-brae,
  And theekit [7] it o'er wi' rashes.

They theekit it o'er wi' rashes green,
  They theekit it o'er wi' heather ;
But the pest cam' frae the burrows-town,
  And slew them baith thegither.

[1] Lovingly.  [2] Begged.  [3] Laughed.
[4] Ebb-tide.  [5] Wizards.  [6] Built.
[7] Thatched.

They thought to lye in Methven kirkyard,
    Amang their noble kin ;
But they maun lye in Stronach haugh,[1]
    To biek forenent the sin.[2]

O Bessie Bell and Mary Gray,
    They war twa bonnie lasses ;
They biggit a bower on yon Burn-brae,
    And theekit it o'er wi' rashes.

### THE SILKIE OF SULE SKERRIE

*In Gaelic tradition seals are represented as human beings
under a spell. When they came ashore they were able to resume
their mortal shape and ride over mountain and moor, turning
billows into dark horses. In the Hebrides the seal-tribe were
believed to be the legendary children of the Kings of Lochlann
(i.e., Scandinavia), who on three full moons of the year changed
into men and chose friends and lovers among mankind.*

An earthly nurrice sits an' sings,
    An' aye she sings : " Bye, lilie-wean ;
Little I ken my bairnis' fathèr,
    Far less the land whar maist he's seen."

Then up there rose at her bed-foot,
    And a grumlie guest was he :
" Here I am, thy bairnis' fathèr,
    Tho' I be not sae comelie.

" Upo' the land I am a man,
    A silkie i' yon' sounding sea ;
An' when I'm far awa' frae land
    My dwelling is in Sule Skerriè."

[1] Water-meadow.          [2] To bask beneath the sun.

" It was nae weel," quoth the young mothèr,
    " It was nae well, indeed," quoth she,
" That the Man-Silkie o' Sule Skerriè
    Should cum an' get a bairn ta me ! "

Now he has taen a purse o' gowd
    An' he has put it on her knee,
Saying : " Gie thou ta me my little son,
    An' tak thee up thy nurrice-fee.

" An' it sall be on a summer's day,
    When the sun is hot on ev'ry stane,
That I will learn my little young son
    Ta swim in the saut sea faem.

" An' thou sall't marry a proud gunnèr,
    An' a proud gunnèr he's sure ta be ;
An' the very first shot that he shoots out
    He'll shoot both my young son an' me."


## LORD DERWENTWATER

*James Radclyffe, Earl of Derwentwater* (1689–1716), *was a gallant and notable figure in the Rebellion which ended in the disastrous encounter at Preston. In* 1715 *a warrant was issued against him, on suspicion of being concerned in intrigues on behalf of the Pretender. He was tried for high treason at Westminster, and beheaded on Tower Hill.*

Our King has wrote a lang letter
    And sealed it ower with gold ;
He sent it to my lord Dunwaters,
    To read it if he could.

He has not sent it with a boy, with a boy,
　　Nor with any Scottish lord ;
But he's sent it with the noblest knight
　　E'er Scotland could afford.

The very first line that my lord did read,
　　He gave a smirkling smile ;
Before he had the half of it read,
　　The tears from his eyes did fall.

" Come saddle to me my horse," he said,
　　" Come saddle to me with speed ;
For I must away to fair London town,
　　For me there was ne'er more need."

Out and spoke his lady gay,
　　In child-bed where she lay :
" I would have you make your will, my lord Dunwaters,
Before you go away."

" I leave to you, my eldest son,
　　My houses and my land ;
I leave to you, my youngest son,
　　Ten thousand pounds in hand.

" I leave to you, my lady gay,—
　　You are my wedded wife,—
I leave to you the third of my estate,
　　That'll keep you in a lady's life."

They had not rode a mile but one,
　　Till his horse fell ower a stane :
" It's a warning good enough," my lord Dunwaters said,
　　" Alive I'll ne'er come hame."

When they came to fair London town,
    Into the courtiers' hall,
The lords and knights in fair London town
    Did him a traitor call.

" A traitor ! a traitor ! " says my lord,
    " A traitor ! how can that be ?
An' it was na for the keeping of five thousand men,
    To fight for King Jamie.

" O all you lords and knights in fair London town,
    Come out and see me die :
O all you lords and knights in fair London town,
    Be kind to my lady.

" There's fifty pounds in my right pocket,
    Divide it to the poor ;
There's other fifty in my left pocket,
    Divide it from door to door."

# PART VI

Now on the barren heath they lie,
Their funeral dirge the eagles cry
And mountain breezes o'er them sigh
Who fought and died for Charlie.

*Jacobite Song.*

*The following songs allude to Charles Stuart, grandson of James II., whose attempt to gain the British Throne in 1745 failed. He is described in a letter written in 1714 by his Protestant Chaplain Charles Leslie, as " Tall, Streight, and clean Limb'd, Slender, yet his bones pretty large : He has a very graceful Mien, walks fast, and his Gate has great Resemblance to his Unkle King Charles II., and the Lines of his Face grow dayly more and more like him. He is always Chearful, but seldom Merry, Thoughtful but not Dejected, and bears his Misfortunes with a visible Magnanimity of Spirit." The Catholics in the Highlands were in hopes that this gallant young Prince would succeed in restoring to them the ancient faith of their forefathers.*

Come boat me o'er, come row me o'er,
Come boat me o'er to Charlie ;
I'll gie John Ross anither bawbee
To ferry me o'er to Charlie.
We'll o'er the water,
We'll o'er the sea,
We'll o'er the water to Charlie ;
Come weel, come wo,
We'll gather and go,
And live or die wi' Charlie.

It's weel I lo'e my Charlie's name,
Though some there be abhor him ;
But O to see Auld Nick gaun hame,
And Charlie's faes before him !

255

We'll o'er the water,
We'll o'er the sea,
We'll o'er the water to Charlie ;
Come weel, come wo,
We'll gather and go,
And live or die wi' Charlie.

I swear by moon and starns sae bright,
And sun that glances early,
If I had twenty thousand lives,
I'd gie them a' for Charlie.
We'll o'er the water,
We'll o'er the sea,
We'll o'er the water to Charlie ;
Come weel, come wo,
We'll gather and go,
And live or die wi' Charlie.

I ance had sons, but now hae nane ;
I bred them toiling sairly ;
And I wad bear them a' again,
And lose them a' for Charlie.
We'll o'er the water,
We'll o'er the sea,
We'll o'er the water to Charlie ;
Come weel, come wo.
We'll gather and go,
And live or die wi' Charlie.

## THE SHEPHERD BOY'S LAMENT

*These lines are said to have been composed by a chivalrous herd-boy, on seeing the men of his clan set out to join Prince Charlie.*

The folks with plaids, the folks with plaids,
The folks with plaids of scarlet,—
And folks with checkered plaids of green
Are going on tour with Charlie.

Were I myself a sixteen-years-old—
Were I as I would fain be ;
Were I myself a sixteen-years-old,
I'd go myself with Charlie.

## CHARLIE IS MY DARLING

'Twas on a Monday morning,
Right early in the year,
That Charlie came to our town,
The young Chevalier.
And Charlie he's my darling,
My darling, my darling,
And Charlie he's my darling,
The young Chevalier.

As Charlie he came up the gate,
His face shone like the day :
I grat to see the lad come back,
That had been lang away.
And Charlie he's my darling, etc., etc.,

And ilka bonny lassie sang,
As to the door she ran,
Our king shall hae his ain again,
And Charlie is the man.
And Charlie he's my darling, etc., etc.

Out owre yon moory mountain,
And down yon craigy glen,
Of naething else our lasses sing,
But Charlie and his men.
And Charlie he's my darling, etc., etc.

Our Highland hearts are true and leal,
And glow without a stain ;
Our Highland swords are metal keen,
And Charlie he's our ain.
And Charlie he's my darling, etc., etc.

*James Hogg*, 1770–1835.

## WAE'S ME FOR PRINCE CHARLIE

*Bird-speech was a very early superstition, and there are many
examples in folk-lore of winged emissaries, who bring warnings
to those who need them. In Eccles. x. 20, we read : " Curse
not the King, no not in thy thought . . . for a bird of the air
shall carry the voice, and that which hath wings shall tell the
matter." This belief is probably founded on the ancient
bird-cult, a religion in which birds were either Gods, or the
medium of communication to man. Popular proverbial lore
has perpetuated the idea of a little songster who carries gossip*

*abroad. In the following verses the loyal bird sings the story
of an outcast Prince and the lost hopes of a faithful people.*

A wee bird came to our ha' door,
He warbled sweet and clearly,
And aye the o'ercome o' his sang,
Was " Wae's me for Prince Charlie ! "
Oh ! when I heard the bonny bonny bird,
The tears came drapping rarely,
I took my bonnet aff my head,
For weel I lo'ed Prince Charlie.

Quo' I, " My bird, my bonny bonny bird,
　Is that a tale ye borrow ?
Or is't some words ye've learnt by rote,
　Or a lilt o' dool and sorrow ? "
" Oh ! no, no, no ! " the wee bird sang,
　" I've flown sin' morning early ;
But sic a day o' wind and rain !
　Oh ! wae's me for Prince Charlie ! "

" On hills that are by right his ain,
　He roams a lonely stranger ;
On ilka hand he's press'd by want,
　On ilka side by danger.
Yestreen I met him in a glen,
　My heart near bursted fairly,
For sadly changed indeed was he,
　Oh ! wae's me for Prince Charlie !

Dark night came on, the tempest howl'd
　Out-owre the hills and valleys ;
And whare was't that your prince lay down,
　Whase hame should been a palace ?

He row'd him in a highland plaid,
    Which cover'd him but sparely,
And slept beneath a bush o' broom,
    Oh ! wae's me for Prince Charlie ! "
But now the bird saw some redcoats,
    And he shook his wings wi' anger ;
O this is no a land for me,
    I'll tarry here nae langer."
A while he hover'd on the wing,
    Ere he departed fairly
But weel I mind the farewell strain ;
    T'was " Wae's me for Prince Charlie ! "

                    *William Glen*, 1789–1826.


                SOMEBODY

" *Somebody," of course, is Charles Stuart. He was known
by this epithet when it was not considered safe to call him by his
full name.*

        My heart is sair, I daurna tell,
        My heart is sair for somebody ;
        I wad walk a winter's night,
        For a sight o' somebody.
        O hon for somebody !
        O hey for somebody !
        I wad do—what wad I not,
        For the sake o' somebody ?

        If somebody were come again,
        Then somebody maun cross the main,
        And ilka ane will get his ane,
        And I will see my somebody.

O hon for somebody !
O hey for somebody !
I wad do—what wad I not,
For the sake o' somebody ?

What need I kame my tresses bright ?
Or why should coal or candle-light
E'er shine in my bower day or night,
Since gane is my dear somebody ?
O hon for somebody !
O hey for somebody !
I wad do—what wad I not,
For the sake o' somebody ?

Oh ! I hae grutten mony a day
For ane that's banish'd far away :
I canna sing, and munna say,
How sair I grieve for somebody ?
O hon for somebody !
O hey for somebody !
I wad do—what wad I not,
For the sake o' somebody ?

*From Cromek's " Remains " (1810).*

## I HAE NAE KITH, I HAE NAE KIN

*This sweet and curious little song is not easily understood. The allusion to the King's daughter shows it to be very ancient. The last verse probably refers to some plot that the Jacobites expected to prove destructive.*

I hae nae Kith, I hae nae Kin,
Nor ane that's dear to me,
For the bonny lad that I love best,
He's far beyond the sea.

He's gone with one that was our own,
And we may rue the day,
When our King's own daughter came here,
To play such foul play.

O gin I were a bonny bird,
With wings that I might flee,
Then I would travel o'er the main,
My own true love to see :
Then I would tell a joyful tale
To one that's dear to me,
And sit upon a King's window,
And sing my melody.

The adder lies in the corbie's [1] nest,
Aneath the Corbie's wame, [2]
And the blast that reaves the corbie's brood
Shall blow our good King hame.
Then blow ye east, or blow ye west,
Or blow ye o'er the faem,
O bring the lad that I love best,
And one I dare not name.

*Anon.*

## BONNY CHARLIE

*This song is said to have been written by Captain Stuart, of Invernahoyle.*

Tho' my fire-side it be but sma',
And bare and com-fort-less with-a',
I'll keep a seat, and may-be twa,
To welcome bon-ny Charlie.

[1] Raven.          [2] Breast.

Although my aumrie and my shiel
Are toom as the glen of Earn-an-hyle,
I'll keep my hindmost hand-fu' meal,
To gie to bon-ny Charlie.

Although my lands are fair and wide,
It's there nae langer I maun bide ;
Yet my last hoof, and horn, and hide,
I'll gie to bonny Charlie.
Although my heart is unco sair,
And lies fu' lowly in its lair,
Yet the last drap o' blude that's there
I'll gie for bonny Charlie.

## THE WIND HAS BLAWN MY PLAID AWAY

Over the hills, an' far away,
It's over the hills, an' far away,
O'er the hills, an' o'er the sea,
The wind has blawn my plaid frae me.
My tartan plaid, my ae good sheet,
That keepit me frae wind an' weet,
An' held me bien baith night an' day,
Is over the hills, an' far away.

There was a wind, it cam to me,
Over the south, an' over the sea,
An' it hath blawn my corn an' hay,
Over the hills an' far away.
It blew my corn, it blew my gear,
It neither left me kid nor steer,
An' blew my plaid, my only stay,
Over the hills an' far away.

But though 't has left me bare indeed,
An' blawn the bonnet off my head,
There's something hid in Highland brae,
It hasna blawn my sword away.
Then over the hills, an' over the dales,
Over all England, an' through Wales,
The braidsword yet shall bear the sway,
Over the hills an' far away.


## IT WAS A' FOR OUR RIGHTFU' KING

*There is a haunting beauty in this song, traditionally said to have been written by a Captain Ogilvie, of Inverquharity, who was with King James on his Irish expedition, and fought at the battle of the Boyne, afterwards voluntarily exiling himself to attend James II. in France. The first two verses are the noble utterances of a brave soldier torn from his love, who in the last wistful lines laments her loneliness, " whilst all the withered world looks drearily, like a dim picture of the drownéd past."*

" It was a' for our rightfu' King
We left fair Scotland's strand,
It was a' for our rightfu' King
We e'er saw Irish land, my dear,
We e'er saw Irish land.

Now a' is done that men can do,
And a' is done in vain :
My love an' native land, fareweel,
For I maun cross tha main, my dear,
For I maun cross the main."

He turned him right an' round about,
Upon the Irish shore,
An' ga'e his bridle-rein a shake,
With, " Adieu for evermore, my dear,"
With, " Adieu for evermore."

" *The sodger frae the wars returns,*
*The sailor frae the main :*
*But I hae parted frae my love,*
*Never to meet again, my dear,*
*Never to meet again.*

*When day is gane, an' night is come,*
*An' a' folk bound to sleep,*
*I think on him that's far awa',*
*The lee-lang night, an' weep, my dear,*
*The lee-lang night, an' weep.*"

# PART VII

An air is more lasting than the voice of the birds,
A word is more lasting than the riches of the world.

*Old Gaelic Proverb.*

DERMID AND GRAINA

*After the Druids, who were the priests and philosophers of
every State where their religion prevailed, the Bards were of all
men the most respected, and for many ages ranked next in
dignity to the King. Their office became hereditary, and their
songs, which had great influence on the manners of the Celtic
tribes, were handed down by tradition. The ancient Cale-
donians were a nation of musicians, and every hero could
" touch the harp and melt the soul." Beda tells us that even
in the seventh century it was customary to pass that instrument
from hand to hand at feasts and entertainments.*

*Ossian, heroic poet of the Gael, was the son of the third century
hero Fingal or Fionn Mac Cumhail. James Mac Pherson claims
to have discovered his poems, and in 1760 published a translation
which excited a storm of controversy which has not yet subsided,
owing to the unsatisfactory statements about his originals. The
following fragments were translated and published by John
Smith, Minister at Kilbrandon, Argyleshire, at Edinburgh in
1780. His faith and enthusiasm may be seen in these lines :
" Most of those poets who have made the greatest figures, were,
like Homer, Shakespeare and Ossian, for the most part indebted
for it to a native fire and enthusiasm of genius, to which,
perhaps, the learning of the schools and the precepts of Aristotle
would have done little service. Poetic talents are entirely the
gift of that universal mother nature, who is not so partial to her
children, as some are apt to suspect her. Trojans or Rutilians
north or south of the Tweed are distinctions unknown to her in
the distribution of her favours. She touches alike the lyre of*

*Homer, and the harp of Ossian, and equally inspires the ode of
the Laplander and the love-song of the Arcadian.*"

" Fair is thy form, my love ; and like the bloom of trees
in spring is thy beauty ; yet this day I must leave thee with
thy child in the cave, and mix with heroes on Golbun."

" And wilt thou leave me," said Graina, " loveliest of men ;
wilt thou leave me, thou light of my soul in darkness ?
Where is my joy but in the face of Dermid ? Where is my
safety but in thy shield of brass ? Wilt thou leave me, thou
fairer than the sun when he smiles after the shower, on the
leaf of the birch ; thou milder than his evening beams, when
they play on the down of the mountain ? Thy son and I
will be sad, if thou art absent, Dermid."

" Graina, dost thou not remember the moan of the crane,
as we wandered early on the hill of our love [1] ? With pity,
thou didst ask the aged son of the rock, Why so sad was the
voice of the crane ? ' Too long,' he replied, ' he hath
stood in the fen ; and the ice hath bound his lazy foot.
Let the idle remember the crane, lest one day they mourn
like him.' Graina, I will not rest longer here. Fingal
might say, with a sigh, ' one of my heroes is become feeble.'
No ; King of Morven, the soul of Dermid is not a stream
that will fail ; the joyful murmur of its course shall always
attend thy steps. Rest thou in thy cave, my love ; with
night I will return with the spoil of roes."

He went, swift as the path of an arrow, when it whistles
thro' the yielding air on its two gray wings. Graina climbed,
pensive and slow, the hill, to view the chase of roes from
her rock. The light of her countenance is dim ; like the

---

[1] Slia gaoil, " the hill of love," is still the proper name of a mountain
near Kintyre, said to have been the residence of these lovers, and to have
received from them its name.

moon in the night of calm, when it moves in silence through the clouds, and seems the darkened shield of a ghost, hung on high in his own airy hall.

### THE VALLEY OF CONA

*And so, in this fragment we see a pleasing land of*
*" Dreams that wave before the half-shut eye,*
*And of gay castles in the clouds that pass,*
*For ever flushing round a summer sky . . ."*

How peaceful, this night, art thou, O vale of Cona ! No voice of thy hounds, no sound of thy harps is heard. The sons of the chase are gone to their rest, and the bed has been made for the bards. The murmur of thy stream, O Cona, is faint : the breeze shakes not the dew from thy bended grass. The gray thistle hangs o'er thy bank its sleepy head ; its hairs are heavy with the drops of night. The roe sleeps, fearless, in the booth of the hunter ; his voice hath ceased to disturb her, and she sees his tomb, amid green ferns, before her. Lightly her little kid leaps o'er its mound, rubbing with his horn the moss from its gray stone ; and on the soft heap, when tired of play, lays himself down to rest. Vale of Cona, how art thou changed ! And thou, hill of Golbun, how quiet is now thy heath ! Thou coverest thy head with thy dark veil of mist ; and slumberest in the noon of day. No voice of the hunter, no cry of the hound, travels along thy dark-brown side to awake thee. Thou art silent, O Golbun, in thy bed of clouds : no voice of thine is heard ; save when thou repliest to the sportive cry of the deer, when evening has half-hid the sun in the wave of the west. Then, dost thou reply : but thy words are few, and thou composest thyself again to thy slumber. How peaceful art thou, O Vale of Cona ! Thy warriors and thy hunters are all gone to rest. Let the bed be also made for the bard ; for the shades of night thicken around him, and his eyes are heavy.

### THE DEAD

The sun, O woods, shall return again ; and your green leaves, in his warm beam, will flourish. The season of your youth will come back, and all your bare boughs will rejoice. From the height of his beauty, the dweller of heaven will look down : he will smile through the thin sparkling shower, on the herbs that are withered. They also will come forth from their winter-house, and lift their green glittering head on the bank of their secret stream. They will come forth from their dark house, with joy : but the dwellers of the tomb remain still in their place ; no warm beam of the sun shall revive them.

*From " Cathula."*

### THE KERTCH [1]

### (A MARRIAGE SONG)

*The following Runes and Incantations were translated by Dr. Carmichael and are to be found in no other book than his " Carmina Gadelica," published in 1900. He was chieftain or*

---

[1] The kertch, or coif, was a square of linen formed into a cap, and donned by a woman on the morning after her marriage. It was the sign of wifehood.

*president of various Gaelic societies, and his influence has been very great over the younger generation of Celtic students and writers.*

A thousand hails to thee beneath thy kertch,
During thy course mayest thou be whole,
Strength and days be thine in peace,
Thy paradise with thy means increase.

In the beginning thy dual race, and thou young,
In beginning thy course, seek thou the God of Life,
Fear not but He will rightly rule
Thine every secret need and prayer.

This spousal crown thou now hast donned,
Full oft has gotten grace to woman,
Be thou virtuous, but be gracious,
Be thou pure in word and hand.

Be thou hospitable, yet be wise,
Be thou courageous, but be calm,
Be thou frank, but be reserved,
Be thou exact, yet generous.

Be not miserly in giving,
Do not flatter, yet be not cold,
Speak not ill of man, though ill he be,
If spoken of, show not resentment.

Be thou careful of thy name,
Be thou dignified yet kind,
The Hand of God be on thine helm,
In inception, in act, and in thought.

Be not querulous beneath thy cross,
Walk thou warily when the cup is full,
Never to evil give thou countenance,
And with thy kertch, to thee a hundred thousand hails !

## POEM OF THE BEETLES

*There are many curious legends current in the Isles about the sacred beetle. When Christ's enemies were searching for him to put him to death, they met the sacred beetle and the grave-digger beetle. The Jews asked the beetles if they had seen Christ passing that way. Proud to be asked, the gravedigger promptly replied : " Yes ! He passed here yesterday," but the sacred beetle said : " You lie ! it was a year ago yesterday that Christ passed by." Therefore the gravedigger is remorse-lessly killed on account of his officiousness in helping to betray Christ, whereas the sacred beetle is always spared, because he desired to save Him.*

When Christ was under the wood,
And enemies were pursuing Him,
The crooked one of deception [1]
Said to the black beetle and the butterfly—

" Saw ye pass to-day or yesterday,
The Son of my love, the Son of God ? "
" We saw ! we saw ! " said the black beetle,
" The Son of redemption pass yesterday."

" False ! false ! false ! "
Said the little clay beetle [2] of horses,
" A full year yesterday,
The Son of God went by."

[1] Judas.                    [2] Sacred beetle.

### THE INCENSE

*This is a world, where we know that nothing is unchangeable, and there is little enough of comfort in these stark lines which have their fitting place next to Obadiah's, " though thou exalt thyself as the eagle, and though thou set thy nest among the stars, thence will I bring thee down, saith the Lord."*

In the day of thy health,
Thou wilt not give devotion,
Thou wilt not give kine,
Nor wilt thou offer incense.

Head of naughtiness,
Heart of greediness,
Mouth unhemmed,
Nor ashamed art thou.

But thy winter will come,
And the hardness of thy distress,
And thy head shall be as
The clod in the earth.

Thy strength having failed,
Thine aspect having gone,
And thou a thrall,
On thy two knees.

*Idem.*

# INDEX OF AUTHORS

# INDEX OF FIRST LINES

# INDEX OF FIRST LINES

I wish I had died my own fair death, 148
If you would lufe and luvit be, 123
*Imprimis.* For ten loads of coal, 162
In a garden so green in a May-morning, 53
In melancholic fancy, 176
In the day of thy health, 275
In the year 1482, no man was to open his booth, 15
In this same year, (1511,) the King of Scotland built a ship, 41
In vain thou look'st that I should show, 173
Into ane garth, under ane reid roseir, 13
It came to that, he keept his chamber still to his death, 190
It is beyond the reach of Man to assign Reasons, 189
It was a' for our rightfu' King, 264

Kiss'd yestreen, and kiss'd yestreen, 164

Lanterne of love, and lady fair of hue, 120
Lo, fair ladies, Cressid of Troy's towne, 12
Lord Jesu Chryst that crounit was with Thornse, 106

Madam, the agreeable accounts of your safe arrival, 201
Madame and dearest sister.—Notwithstanding of my, 112
Maister.—I haif received diverse letters from you, 75
March said to Aperill, 93
May the hinges of friendship ne'er rust, 218
Maydens of Englande, sore may ye morne, 6
Monsieur mon bon frère, 74
Most noble lady, it is not without reason, 43
My dear heart, bless the Lord on my behalf, 188
My dear Sir, Here I am, and Mr. Samuel Johnson, 202
My heart is sair, I daurna tell, 260
My Lord, I have seen now all, 164
My Lord, I recommend my hearty service onto your Lordship, 47
My lute, be as thou wast when thou didst grow, 132
My most dear lord and father, 36
My prince in God gife thee guid grace, 35

Now fair, fairest of every fair, 32
Now is it that the mindes of men are qualified, 142
Now leif thy mirth, now leif thy haill plesance, 31
Now that death hath thus disposed of the late French King, 63

O Bessie Bell and Mary Gray, 248
O ! do not kill that bee, 135
O duilfull death ! O dragon dolorous ! 40
O happie death, to life the readie way, 105
O ! lang, lang is the winter nicht, 225
O Lord, we acknowledge that no creature is able, 58
O man, rise up, and be not sweir, 122

281

O Mater Dei, 56
O Perfect Light, which shaid away, 101
O waly, waly up the bank, 151
" O whar hae ye been, my lang, lang love," 244
" O whare are ye gaun ? " 231
O whare gang ye, thou silly old carle ? 234
O where were ye, my milk-white steed, 159
Of this fair volume which we world do name, 135
On Sunday, being the thirtieth of July, 1587..88
Once in the year, which is the whole month of August, 145
Our King has wrote a lang letter, 250
Over the hills, an' far away, 263

PRAISE yee Jehovah, nations all, 141

QUHEN Alysandyr oure King was dede, 3
Quod te jampridem videt, ac amat absens, 76

REJOIS thairfoir my half in all, 107
Return hamewart my heart again, 68
Right traist friend, we grete you heartilie weel, 114
Robert Melwyne.—Ye shall not fail to send, 73

SEN throw vertew incressis dignitie, 10
She sat down below a thorn, 241
Sir, I heard very much, but believed very little, 193
Sir John he got him an ambling nag, 229
Sir, Your antient and native kingdom of Scotland, 168
Sleep, Silence' child, sweet father of soft rest, 134
So suete a kis yistrene fra thee I reft, 97
Stay not away because thou, and the gift thou offerest, 156
Stay passenger, take notice, 183
Suete Nichtingale in holene grene that han[ts], 98
Sweet, sweet brother, I thank you for your letter, 143
Syr, I have receaved yours, 175

TAK time in time, or time be tint, 99
Than turnis he his sail anon, 9
That poor silly Jeezabel, our Queen Mary, married, 77
The countrie of Scotland shee esteemed not soe farr, 63
The daughter of debate, that eke discord doth sow, 77
The devil in man's likeness met her going out, 111
The earth goes on the earth glittering in gold, 205
The folks with plaids, the folks with plaids, 257
The gardener stands in his bower door, 96
The God of mercies grant you a full gale and a fair entry, 188
The Gowans are gay, my jo, 54
The King is 25 years and some months old, 27
The King sent his lady on the first Yule day, 185

PRINTED IN GREAT BRITAIN BY THE WHITEFRIARS PRESS, LTD.,
LONDON AND TONBRIDGE.